...where the Spirit of the Lord is,
there is freedom.

2 Corinthians 3:17

Melchizedek Consciousness Volume 2

Activating the Mind of Christ

Adonijah O. Ogbonnaya, Ph.D.

Publications Copyright @ 2025, literature arm of AACTEV8 International
(Apostolic Activation Network) Aactev8 International
1020 Victoria Ave.
Venice, CA 90291
www.aactev8.com

Published by Seraph Creative

Library of Congress data

The American Standard Version (ASV) is used for all scripture references unless otherwise noted.

Italics in scripture are added by the author.
Editor: Kathy Strecker

Cover art, Typesetting, Illustration & Layout by Feline Graphics
www.felinegraphics.com

Melchizedek Conciousness

Volume Two

Activating the Mind of Christ

Dr. Adonijah Ogbonnaya Ph.D.

ACKNOWLEDGEMENTS

Although it is possible to write a book like this one by oneself, it is not necessarily advisable or wise. What we do is for the benefit of humankind and involves the energy of humanity to bring it to fruition. If it were not for the loving input and care of the many people around me, this book would not exist—at least not at this time. It is their love, care, and dedication that has made this work possible while giving me freedom to pursue other areas of research and teaching without being stuck. All the ideas in this book, along with their success or failure to please the reader, are mine. However, I would be remiss if I did not express my gratitude for the work done by many others to bring it to publication.

I thank my publisher, Seraph Creative and the team, Linda Lurie and Leigh Brett. I am grateful to Kathy Strecker who edited the book, Ronald Montijn who transcribed and did some editing of the manuscript, and John Eichelberger who read and offered input on the second draft.

I am especially grateful for my hard-working staff, Edward Johnson and Monique Tyson, who coordinate my publications and do so much to help keep them on track.

I thank the Melchizedek Church of Nashville, Pastor Donald Crossland, and all the staff who gave me the opportunity to teach this material to the church before I wrote the book. Thanks to all my students who study with me. Our interactions allow me to seek deeper places of relationship and cultivate more openness to new depths of revelatory knowledge from the Word.

My deepest thanks and gratitude are for the Word Made Flesh, Yeshua, our Lord and Master, who deserves all glory and honor. AMEN!

Adonijah Ogbonnaya
Lake Elsinore, CA
2024

Contents

Chapter 1

WHO IS MELCHIZEDEK?

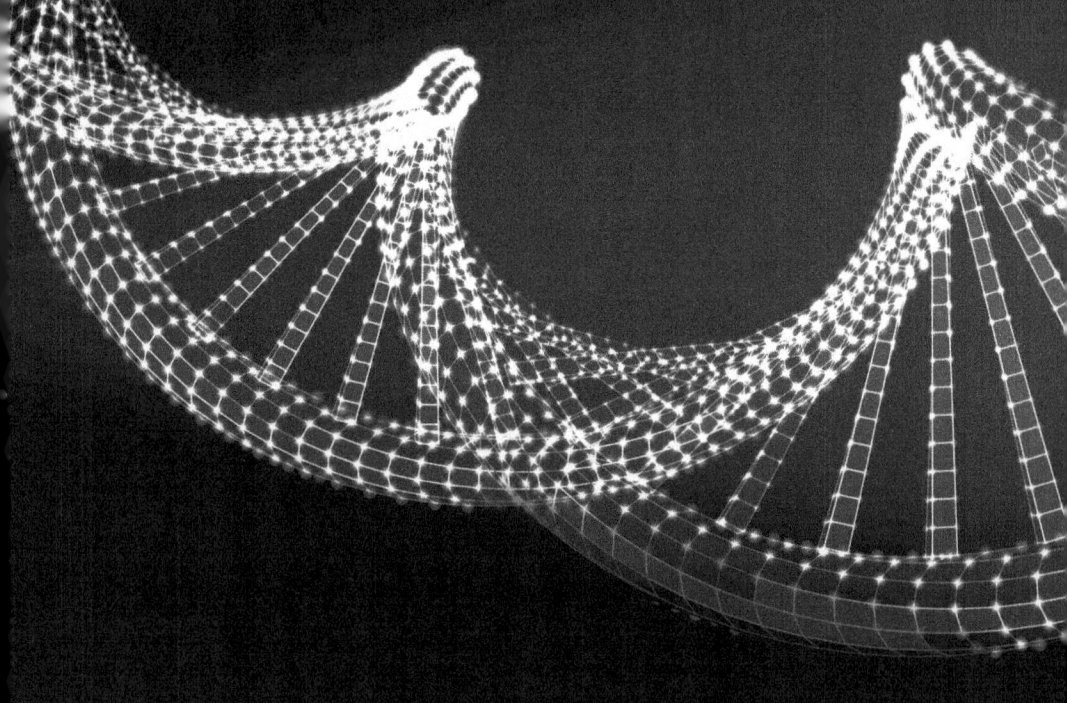

Melchizedek has fascinated the church since its early days, but even more so, has fascinated Israel from the days of Abraham, to their stay in Egypt, and throughout their history. There are different perspectives on who Melchizedek is so I will spend some time laying the foundation.

It is important to know that there is more written about Melchizedek outside of the Bible than there is within it. Many of the books written by the Rabbis, such as the Genesis Rabbah,[1] Leviticus Rabbah, Numbers Rabbah, or other ancient commentaries on scripture, have much to say about Melchizedek. Even the apocryphal book of Ezra and the second book of Enoch[2] have passages about Melchizedek. However, the principle of Melchizedek is something that believers must understand, as scripture is clear on its importance. Despite arguments from Levites and sons of Levi about the superiority of our priesthood, it is only when we understand Melchizedek that our priesthood makes sense.

Melchizedek blessed Abraham, and in the old period, the greater blesses the lesser and the lesser gives thanks. The one with something blesses the other. Responding with "Bless you, too" is not the same as giving a blessing, which is what the Bible teaches. We have developed a terrible habit of not saying thank you when someone blesses us. Instead, we throw the blessing back to them, "Bless you, too!" We do not take the time to receive the blessing. I am trying to work on that myself now. If someone says, "Bless you," I say, "Thank you, I receive the blessing," instead of turning around and saying, "Bless you, too!"

Let us begin by looking at how scripture talks about Melchizedek before getting into all the nuances, especially as it relates to us as believers. We may touch briefly on the Aaronic priesthood, as that is what the writer of Hebrews does.

1   Bereshit Rabbah is a talmudic-era midrash on the Book of Genesis. It covers most of the book (excluding genealogies and similar passages) with verse-by-verse and often word-by-word commentary. Written in Hebrew mixed with Aramaic and occasional Greek words, its style is simple and clear.

2   2 Enoch 69-73

Three passages in scripture outline the principles of Melchizedek and they are quite brief. Let us start with the first one, and we will refer to it repeatedly. I will quote from other works, but I also want to share revelations about who Melchizedek is because I believe that we must still use the texts, and not just talk about ourselves. We begin in Genesis 14:

> And it came to pass in the days of Amraphel king of Shinar, Arioch king of Ellasar, Chedorlaomer king of Elam, and Tidal king of Goiim, that they made war with Bera king of Sodom, and with Birsha king of Gomorrah, Shinab king of Admah, and Shemeber king of Zeboiim, and the king of Bela (the same is Zoar). All these joined together in the vale of Siddim (the same is the Salt Sea).

> Twelve years they served Chedorlaomer, and in the thirteenth year, they rebelled. And in the fourteenth year came Chedorlaomer, and the kings that were with him, and smote the Rephaim in Ashteroth-karnaim, and the Zuzim in Ham, and the Emim in Shaveh-kiriathaim, and the Horites in their mount Seir, unto El-paran, which is by the wilderness. And they returned and came to En-mishpat (the same is Kadesh), and smote all the country of the Amalekites, and also the Amorites, that dwelt in Hazazon-tamar.

> And there went out the king of Sodom, and the king of Gomorrah, and the king of Admah, and the king of Zeboiim, and the king of Bela (the same is Zoar); and they set the battle in array against them in the vale of Siddim; against Chedorlaomer king of Elam, and Tidal king of Goiim, and Amraphel king of Shinar, and Arioch king of Ellasar; four kings against the five.

Now the vale of Siddim was full of slime pits; and the kings of Sodom and Gomorrah fled, and they fell there, and they that remained fled to the mountain. And they took all the goods of Sodom and Gomorrah, and all their victuals, and went their way. And they took Lot, Abram's brother's son, who dwelt in Sodom, and his goods, and departed.

And there came one that had escaped and told Abram the Hebrew: now he dwelt by the oaks of Mamre, the Amorite, brother of Eshcol, and brother of Aner; and these were confederate with Abram.

And when Abram heard that his brother was taken captive, he led forth his trained men, born in his house, three hundred and eighteen, and pursued as far as Dan. And he divided himself against them by night, he and his servants, and smote them, and pursued them unto Hobah, which is on the left hand of Damascus.

And he brought back all the goods, and also brought back his brother Lot, and his goods, and the women also, and the people.

And the king of Sodom went out to meet him, after his return from the slaughter of Chedorlaomer and the kings that were with him, at the vale of Shaveh (the same is the King's Vale). And Melchizedek king of Salem brought forth bread and wine: and he was priest of God Most High.

And he blessed him, and said, Blessed be Abram of God Most High, possessor of heaven and earth: and blessed be God Most High, who hath delivered thine enemies into thy hand. And he gave him a tenth of all.

And the king of Sodom said unto Abram, Give me the persons, and take the goods to thyself. And Abram said to the king of Sodom, I have lifted up my hand unto Jehovah, God Most High, possessor of heaven and earth, that I will not take a thread nor a shoe-latchet nor aught that is thine, lest thou shouldest say, I have made Abram rich: save only that which the young men have eaten, and the portion of the men that went with me, Aner, Eshcol, and Mamre; let them take their portion. (Genesis 14:1-24)

We also read Psalm 110, which talks about Melchizedek:

Jehovah saith unto my Lord, Sit thou at my right hand, Until I make thine enemies thy footstool. Jehovah will send forth the rod of thy strength out of Zion: Rule thou in the midst of thine enemies.

Thy people offer themselves willingly In the day of thy power, in holy array: Out of the womb of the morning, Thou hast the dew of thy youth.

Jehovah hath sworn and will not repent: Thou art a priest forever After the order of Melchizedek.

The Lord at thy right hand Will strike through kings in the day of his wrath. He will judge among the nations, He will fill the places with dead bodies; He will strike through the head in many countries. He will drink of the brook in the way: Therefore will he lift up the head. (Psalm 110)

Now we are going to read an important scripture from Hebrews 5:

> For every High Priest, being taken from among men, is appointed for men in things pertaining to God, that he may offer both gifts and sacrifices for sins: who can bear gently with the ignorant and erring, for that he himself also is compassed with infirmity; and by reason thereof is bound, as for the people, so also for himself, to offer for sins. And no man taketh the honor unto himself, but when he is called of God, even as was Aaron. So Christ also glorified not himself to be made a High Priest, but he that spake unto him,
>
> Thou art my Son,
>
> This day have I begotten thee:
>
> as he saith also in another place,
>
> Thou art a priest forever
>
> After the order of Melchizedek.
>
> Who in the days of his flesh, having offered up prayers and supplications with strong crying and tears unto him that was able to save him from death, and having been heard for his godly fear, though he was a Son, yet learned obedience by the things which he suffered; and having been made perfect, he became unto all them that obey him the author of eternal salvation; named of God a High Priest after the order of Melchizedek. Of whom we have many things to say, and hard of interpretation, seeing ye are become dull of hearing.
>
> For when by reason of the time ye ought to be teachers, ye have need again that someone teach you

the rudiments of the first principles of the oracles
of God; and are become such as have need of milk,
and not of solid food. For every one that partaketh
of milk is without experience of the word of
righteousness; for he is a babe. (Hebrews 5:1-13)

This passage is important because in those days, people
would offer milk and other provisions to strangers who came
into their presence. However, Melchizedek offered wine
to Abraham. It is worth reading again because there is an
implicit comparison being made.

For every one that partaketh of milk is without
experience of the word of righteousness; for he is a
babe. But solid food is for fullgrown men, even those
who by reason of use have their senses exercised to
discern good and evil. (Hebrews 5:13-14)

Do you see the point? Now let us read from Hebrews 6:

For when God made promise to Abraham,
since he could swear by none greater, he sware by
himself, saying, Surely blessing I will bless thee, and
multiplying I will multiply thee. And thus, having
patiently endured, he obtained the promise. For men
swear by the greater: and in every dispute of theirs
the oath is final for confirmation.

Wherein God, being minded to show more
abundantly unto the heirs of the promise the
immutability of his counsel, interposed with an
oath; that by two immutable things, in which it
is impossible for God to lie, we may have a strong
encouragement, who have fled for refuge to lay
hold of the hope set before us: which we have as an

anchor of the soul, a hope both sure and stedfast and entering into that which is within the veil; whither as a forerunner Jesus entered for us, having become a High Priest for ever after the order of Melchizedek.

For this Melchizedek, king of Salem, priest of God Most High, who met Abraham returning from the slaughter of the kings and blessed him, to whom also Abraham divided a tenth part of all (being first, by interpretation, King of righteousness, and then also King of Salem, which is, King of peace; without father, without mother, without genealogy, having neither beginning of days nor end of life, but made like unto the Son of God), abideth a priest continually.

Now consider how great this man was, unto whom Abraham, the patriarch, gave a tenth out of the chief spoils. And they indeed of the sons of Levi that receive the priest's office have commandment to take tithes of the people according to the law, that is, of their brethren, though these have come out of the loins of Abraham: but he whose genealogy is not counted from them hath taken tithes of Abraham, and hath blessed him that hath the promises.

But without any dispute the less is blessed of the better. And here men that die receive tithes; but there one, of whom it is witnessed that he liveth. And, so to say, through Abraham, even Levi, who receiveth tithes, hath paid tithes; for he was yet in the loins of his father when Melchizedek met him.

Now if there was perfection through the Levitical priesthood (for under it hath the people received the law), what further need was there that another priest should arise after the order of Melchizedek, and not be reckoned after the order of Aaron? For the priesthood being changed, there is made of necessity a change also of the law. For he of whom these things are said belongeth to another tribe, from which no man hath given attendance at the altar. For it is evident that our Lord hath sprung out of Judah; as to which tribe Moses spake nothing concerning priests. And what we say is yet more abundantly evident, if after the likeness of Melchizedek there ariseth another priest, who hath been made, not after the law of a carnal commandment, but after the power of an endless life: for it is witnessed of him,

Thou art a priest forever

After the order of Melchizedek.

For there is a disannulling of a foregoing commandment because of its weakness and unprofitableness (for the law made nothing perfect), and a bringing in thereupon of a better hope, through which we draw nigh unto God. And inasmuch as it is not without the taking of an oath (for they indeed have been made priests without an oath; but he with an oath by him that saith of him, The Lord sware and will not repent himself, Thou art a priest forever); by so much also hath Jesus become the surety of a better covenant. And they indeed have been made priests many in number, because that by death they are hindered from continuing: but he, because he abideth forever, hath his priesthood unchangeable. Wherefore also he is able to save to the uttermost them that draw near unto God through him, seeing he ever liveth to make intercession for them. For such a High Priest became us, holy, guileless, undefiled, separated

from sinners, and made higher than the heavens; who needeth not daily, like those High Priests, to offer up sacrifices, first for his own sins, and then for the sins of the people: for this he did once for all, when he offered up himself. For the law appointeth men High Priests, having infirmity; but the word of the oath, which was after the law, appointeth a Son, perfected forevermore. (Hebrews 6:13 - 7:28)

That is a remarkable promise! It is good to read the text. Some people claim that Melchizedek was the king of present-day Jerusalem, but this is not the case. By the time the Israelites reached the Jebusite site, Jerusalem had become a center of sickness and all kinds of unsavory things. Even the Jebusites stated that David could not enter the city due to the rampant disease and sickness.[3] Therefore, from the outset, we must look at Melchizedek from a different perspective. There are several tales about Melchizedek, but we will examine ours from a unique viewpoint.

First, some argue that Melchizedek was simply a human being with no record of his existence. However, the scripture does not support this claim. The scripture states that he was without father or mother and had no genealogy. This is a crucial point. No genetic lineage on earth can be traced back to Melchizedek, and we will discuss the reasons for this later.

Saying that Melchizedek is merely an ordinary human being creates a problem. No ordinary human lives forever and serves as a priest eternally. The mysteries surrounding Melchizedek are important for those who believe and are now part of the Order of Melchizedek as followers of Christ.

---

3   2 Samuel 5:6

Secondly, another aspect of Melchizedek that is sometimes misunderstood is the mention of him in the Book of Enoch. In fact, there are a number of extra-biblical sources that talk about two Melchizedeks. In the Book of Noah,[4] there is a powerful story. Noah's brother Nir's wife becomes pregnant without Nir ever having a relationship with her, and she gives birth to a child with the mark of the priesthood on his chest — shining stones embedded in his chest. The people run out to see if this child is one of the Watchers and their creations. However, according to that text, God sent a messenger to let them know that this child is Melchizedek and that another Melchizedek will come in the future. As stated earlier, there is more about Melchizedek in extra-biblical texts than there is in scripture itself, as there has been a deliberate effort to obscure and overlook the priesthood of Melchizedek. The reasons for this are open to interpretation.

Now, that child, the text says, was born to the mother without the father's involvement, which is a reminder of the later birth of Jesus Christ. The text also states that God gave Noah the message about the flood and this child was taken from earth. God assigned Michael the archangel to take the child to paradise for grooming. It is said that Abraham met this same Melchizedek. I am not explaining the mysteries yet; I am just presenting the argument. But keep in mind that this is a story that happened before the flood, so Melchizedek, according to the story, existed in a pre-diluvian, pre-flood priesthood. There was a priesthood at that time, and Noah and his family were part of it. The birth of this child was within the context of that priesthood, and he had to be taken away to paradise before returning to earth.

---

4   NOAH, BOOK OF. An ancient Jewish work about Noah, known to us from Jubilees (see 10:13; 21:10) and now thought prob. to underlie certain portions of the Book of Enoch (1 Enoch).

I am not saying it is this way, but I want to show you the different possibilities for his origin and identity. The Book of Noah says that this is what happened in the beginning, but it also states that another Melchizedek will come in the end of days.

This story shows that the ancient people, or at least those after David, were speculating and talking about the Melchizedek principle even then. The anticipation of the Messiah was also the anticipation of the entrance of Melchizedek, and the movement of humanity from death to immortality. It was an anticipation of a priesthood where there is no death. So hold that thought.

Melchizedek and Shem

The third point that you can learn from other sources is the argument that Melchizedek was Shem, but the texts do not support that claim. It is supposed that Melchizedek was still alive when Shem was still alive during the time of Abraham, which may be true, but keep in mind that there are missing pieces in the genealogy, and some people are left out, so there is no way Shem could be Melchizedek.

Many people, including some rabbis, have argued that Melchizedek was Shem. This argument arises from the Book of Noah, which states that Melchizedek was born before the flood. However, there is still much confusion surrounding Melchizedek's identity. One thing that is clear, according to the scriptures, is that Melchizedek is without genealogy, having no father or mother and that he holds an eternal priesthood.[5]

5　　Hebrews 7:3

The scriptures also teach that Jesus Christ, born of a woman, is a priest after the order of Melchizedek.[6] This is significant because Jesus cannot be a priest in the Levitical Order. The Bible says that Jesus Christ was born under the law to fulfill it,[7] supersede it, and become the one who re-establishes a priesthood that is not based on Israel.

Now, let us look at this more closely. This is important because Melchizedek, whom Abraham met, was a Gentile in practical terms. He was a Gentile who gave Abraham bread and wine. This Gentile held a superior priesthood, the priesthood of El Elyon, for he was a priest of the nations. There were priesthoods established long before the Aaronic priesthood. For example, Jethro, Moses' father-in-law, was a priest of Midian to God.[8] There is no mention in the scriptures that Jethro was an idol worshipper. God covered over the priesthood that had been established previously because the Gentiles had turned to idolatry, and the knowledge of the one true God was being suppressed by idol worship. This priesthood still existed, but it was truncated and kept away because of idol worship. It was only reinstated and reinvigorated through the coming of the Lord Jesus Christ.

In order to understand this, we need to go back to the person of Christ. And this is what the author of the book of Hebrews does. He takes us back to the priesthood of Melchizedek, which was for the entire world long before there was an Israel. It was a global priesthood. Melchizedek was the one who managed the heavenly city that was manifested in creation. Remember, Abraham was looking for that city which was on earth and which left the earth and which shall return to the earth.

6 Hebrews 7:1-10; Hebrews 5:10

7 Galatians 4:4

8 Exodus 3:1

The word Melchizedek is "Melchi" which means "my king" and "tsedek" which means "righteousness." The real meaning of the word Melchizedek is "My king is righteousness" not "The king of righteousness." The word is not "Melek-zedek"; it is "Melchi-zedek" which again means "My king is righteousness." So within Melchizedek, there is an embodied principle of righteousness.

Interestingly, the word "tsedek," which means righteousness, is also the name for Jupiter. In the days of Abraham, according to those who have studied astronomy, Jupiter would have been one of the brightest lights in the sky in our galactic system. At that time, just like people today use Venus to orient themselves, travelers used Jupiter to orient themselves during their travel.

So, this planetary system referred to as "tsadek" or "tzadik," which shone in the sky and was used to orient people, was important in the days of Abraham. It was used to show people their way to their destination. It is important for you to remember what orientation means and that it was used to guide people to their destination. In every age that comes around, a particular star ascends to an orientation that allows it to function as a guide. With this understanding, we can see why Jupiter was prominent in so much cultural folklore around the world. In fact, it was prominent in Greece, India, Africa, among the Egyptians, and even among the Jews. Thus, the word for Jupiter became synonymous with righteousness. It represents true North, true righteousness, or a directive towards our destiny. So when Jesus says, "I am the way, the truth, and the life," you need to think of Melchizedek meaning "My King is righteousness" and the orientation towards our destiny. He is not talking only about acts of righteousness, but a *directive towards righteousness*.

This holds many mysteries. I have told you before that if you look at the story of Noah in the Book of Enoch, in the antediluvian and post-diluvian periods which were many centuries later, you will understand that the priesthood God established before the world was created was the reason God created Adam and preserved a genealogy through Noah. Without understanding this, it is difficult to argue for the Levites or Aaron serving as priests. Aaron was a priest because there was already a priestly line, but his process was temporized to accommodate the dying process that had invaded humanity. Remember my previous teaching on the garments of Melchizedek[9] where I argued that the garments Aaron wore kept him alive because they were patterned after the Melchizedek garment? The priest in the garment was not Melchizedek, but the garment kept him alive. In fact, God had to tell Moses and the others, "Take Aaron up to the mountain and take off his garment so that he may die."[10] That is the Melchizedek garment. It ensured that as long as it was worn, the wearer could not die because it was a direct replication of what was seen in heaven. The same is true for the Ark and the Temple, which were both direct replications of what Moses saw in heaven.

If objects on Earth that are mere images contain power, imagine how much more powerful the real thing in heaven is. According to the Book of Revelation, a temple in heaven contains all of these things.[11] Moses was brought there to see and experience them and also served as a representation of Melchizedek. He stood outside the Aaronic priesthood to consecrate it and allow Melchizedek to open up a dimension of ministration to God that only he could do.

---

9   See aactev8.com for more information
10   Numbers 20:28
11   Revelations 11:19

We often hear that Jesus Christ is the Lamb of God, slain from the foundation of the world. But who slew Him, and to whom did He commit His life before the world was created so that He could become the pre-foundation of creation? The answer lies in the mystery of Melchizedek. For if Christ became human and entered into the Order of Melchizedek, then Melchizedek must have been a prototypical human being, as only humans can either offer or be the sacrifice. Melchizedek was the prototypical human being who existed before the creation of Adam and in the mind of God. Even though man had not been created yet, the being of Melchizedek was real. When the Son was needed to create the world and sacrifice His life, the Father could not do it because it is forbidden in scripture for fathers to sacrifice their children. In fact, God put a law against it, and when Abraham could have done it, God stopped him, illustrating that the Father should not sacrifice the Son. The Father can give the Son, but only by the will of the Son, not by sacrificing Him.

Again, the falsehood that we often teach, that the Father killed Jesus, is not true. The Father did not kill Jesus. Human beings acting as priests performed the sacrifice when He died on the cross. Similarly, Melchizedek is the being that stood at the first offering of the Son, the Lamb, before creation, causing the light of the life of the Lamb to flow and to frame creation according to the interior design of the God of heaven and earth. As we move through this material, we need to keep this in mind because "forever" means forever, and "eternal" means eternal. What was God's original intent for humanity? The original intent of God for humanity was for human beings to live forever, with an eternal intent. The fall of man does not change the fact that God's original intent for humanity was to be an ever-living being.

And so, the ever-living being, or archetypal being, before creation must have been a priest because only a priest can make that sacrifice. And if Melchizedek is a priest forever, then when we read about the Lamb of God sacrificed before the foundation of the world, we realize that the sacrifice had to be made from the projective process in the mind of God, whereby the being of man stood over the Lamb of God and slew Him so that the universe could come into existence within the context of the space that God made within himself.

This is important for you as we proceed because that first sacrifice created the universe. And it must be the same sacrifice that comes into the world to redeem the universe. As was the creation, so is the redemption.

Who then is Melchizedek? From what I have experienced, I see that the principle of Melchizedek is manifested in creation at many points. Its final manifestation, which allows all those who believe to become part of the Melchizedek Order, is in the person of Christ. In the beginning, Melchizedek is the one without a father or mother. He is not Jesus Christ. Now, Christ has become a High Priest according to the Melchizedek Order so that archetypal, pre-humanity is now embodied in the person of Christ.

When God became a human being and regained the Melchizedek principle and garment, the garment became fully intertwined with the person of Christ. The body of Christ in which we participate is also part of participating in the Melchizedek principle and body because we are also part of the priesthood. The passage in Hebrews[12] says that Christ brought many people under the priesthood of Melchizedek. Throughout history, the Melchizedek archetypal garment of a human being has manifested in different cultures and

12 Hebrews 7-10

people have gotten to know God because of that. It is a global, eternal priesthood that was covered up by the rise of idolatry. One could also argue that when Melchizedek gave Abraham wine and bread, he initiated Abraham into the Melchizedek Order, which is why communion continues to be a way to reinsert a human being's consciousness into the original intent of God. In contrast, the Aaronic priesthood was exclusively the possession of the people of Israel, although it should not have been because the priests were meant to minister to anyone who came to them. God created the priesthood so that Israel could be a priesthood that ministered to the world.

Melchizedek is a pre-creation reality who became the creation that handles things for God. Melchizedek was a projective image of the eternal principle that God wanted and used. In the temple of heaven, which existed before the creation of the Son and was described in the book of Revelation, man as a divine idea was functioning to sustain the temple according to the pattern of God. If there was no man doing that, Moses would not have come down to ordain Aaron to serve in a temple. So, Melchizedek is about the destiny of all humanity combined and conjoined, when it comes out from under the weight of idolatry and becomes the full manifestation under the eternal High Priest, Jesus Christ, who has become a priest after the Order of Melchizedek.

"Melchi-Zedek" means "My King is Righteousness," and the writer of Hebrews says, "he is also king of Salem, that is, king of peace" (Hebrews 7: 2). The reference to the king of Salem is important because it tells us very clearly that the priesthood of Melchizedek is about kingship and sonship. It is also about a continual upholding of creation according to the pattern of God. It is about initiation into mysteries — the mysteries of life, creation, and redemption. It is very important that we understand that it is about mysteries of framing energetic systems for the manifestation of the intent of God, creating spiritual technologies that manifest the intent of God in creation.

How did Melchizedek know that by giving Abraham communion, the whole DNA of Abraham would change and he would become the bearer of the Messiah? How did he use ordinary bread and wine to change someone's DNA, to transmute that person's DNA, which of course, the Lord Jesus repeats before He goes to the cross?

The first person to do that was Melchizedek. He changed the whole structure of Abraham's being. From that moment on, Abraham began to behave differently, see differently, and function differently. And so, Abraham became a member of the Order of Melchizedek. There is a list of people who served in this way and were not part of the Aaronic priesthood.

In passing, I want to say that the priesthood of Melchizedek comes with an incredible array of wealth because it is a priesthood of kingship. He was the king of the city of Salem. David understood this, and the person he was speaking to was Solomon, who functioned as a priest because he made the sacrifice in the temple. It is amazing to consider the fact that in the account of Solomon making a sacrifice in the temple, the High Priest is not mentioned. Throughout Solomon's reign, the presence of a High Priest is seldom noted. This leads one to believe that Solomon became a representation or embodiment of the priesthood of Melchizedek, being king, priest, and son.

In the Garden of Eden, there was no sacrifice because there was no death. However, Adam still performed a similar role, mediating between creation and its Creator, and creating energetic structures that allowed creation to focus its attention on the Holy One. It is fascinating to consider the idea that Melchizedek was a prototypical human being and may have been *Adam Kadmon*, or the "pre-Adam" Adam. This being embodied the divine principles that God intended to place in Adam. Melchizedek was the directive divine principle that existed before the creation of the world and was the source of all creation when the life of the Lamb was released.

It is also important to note that humanity played a significant role in the sacrifice of Christ. If humanity was responsible for sacrificing Christ, then we are the actual priests that God created. If we were not so divided and tribal, we would have priests that follow the true humanity and serve as ministers of the Most High God. Another interesting point to consider is that God does not act on earth without the involvement of humanity. Humans must submit to God and become a channel for His manifestation in creation. Otherwise, God waits until He finds a human being to work through.

The Melchizedek Order is a real concept. When discussing El Elyon, the Most High God, we must remember that Melchizedek was ministering to the true God, not just one deity among many. In the ancient world, there were priests who were recognized by God and who were part of a pattern of priesthood that was distinct from the Levitical or Aaronic priesthoods. One such priest was Balaam who, even though he was a rogue, was still recognized as a priest-prophet of God.

The Melchizedek Priesthood represents the Order of Humanity, where all individuals initiated into this Order have a direct experience of God, a direct encounter with

God, and a direct connection to God. This Order has been submerged and covered up by idolatry. When a person comes to the consciousness of the Melchizedek Order, before or after the coming of Christ, they receive a revelation of who Christ is and operate in accordance with the Most High God, not an idol. Similarly, when a priest in a particular tribe or place comes to this consciousness, they will also receive this revelation.

Idolatry has submerged and covered the Melchizedek principle that was once embedded in humanity. This turning away from the Most High and toward worshiping created things has led to the suppression of this principle. I believe that the Melchizedek genes were embedded in humanity, but idolatry has taken control. When these genes are unleashed, humanity's consciousness of God or spiritual consciousness will explode.

I also believe that we have reached the age when the gene that was originally embedded in Adam and then initiated into Abraham will be unlocked. The gene found in Noah was the Melchizedek gene, as it says in Genesis 6:9:

Noah was a righteous man, blameless in his generation.

The phrase "my king is righteousness" speaks to the original intent of God for humanity. When this genetic structure is unlocked, a flood of divine consciousness will come into humanity. In reality, there is a Melchizedek gene hidden within humanity. Unfortunately, it continues to be suppressed by idolatry and may become so submerged that it practically disappears from humanity's behavior. This is a shame because the Melchizedek principle has the potential to bring about a significant change in humanity's spiritual

consciousness. In Judaism, you cannot be a priest without having the proper genealogy. Similarly, the Melchizedek human gene runs through humanity and, when activated, allows humanity to be initiated into Divinity.

It is important to note that Melchizedek, who initiated Abraham into the priesthood of El Elyon, was not a Jew, an Israelite, or even a Hebrew. In Genesis 14:19 when Melchizedek said to Abraham, "Blessed be Abram of God Most High," it was a statement of initiation. Melchizedek then sealed this initiation by giving him bread and wine.

When humanity becomes what God intends it to be, the tribal priesthood will submit to the priesthood of Melchizedek, which is the Order of Humanity. In order to become a priest after the Order of Melchizedek, Jesus submitted himself to humanity. Likewise, at the Last Supper, Jesus initiated another group of humanity into the Melchizedek Priesthood by repeating the act of giving bread and wine. This communion was the activation of the Melchizedek principle at that time.

The statement "You are My Son, Today have I begotten You" (Hebrews 5:5; Hebrews 1:5; Psalm 2:7) is often interpreted as the day of Jesus Christ's resurrection or baptism, but this day is not a day in time. It is a Melchizedek day, a day out of time, which represents true humanity that surpasses death and enters into the eternal process. Melchizedek is a representation of us because we all have the potential to become eternal beings. Jesus Christ was initiated into our order and became our High Priest. He learned obedience through the things he suffered, and through his sacrifice, he entered the Order of Melchizedek, the eternal order of humanity intended by God.

Note that Melchizedek was not an ordinary human being, but an eternal being. The eternal gene of Melchizedek is embedded in humanity, allowing us to raise our consciousness of who we are in God to a level of Divinity and eternity. The rise of the Melchizedek Priesthood, and the rise of this consciousness, is the rise of the construct of immortality entering into human life and the world. It is the release of the gene of immortality and the release of all that it represents. We will explore this further in our discussion.

The Melchizedek principle, before creation, released the light and life of the Lamb to cause creation to be manifested. The strands of light moved into creation for it to receive light and life and become a reality. Adam was a manifestation of the Melchizedek Order principle because he served as the mediating principle between creation and the Creator, as well as between the world of the thoughts of God and the world of creation and its manifestation in this world. Before becoming human, Christ the Son of God was the source or the word that created the world. However, the mediator has to be a human being, so the Son became human to participate in that original priesthood and sustain it eternally with the life of God. When Christ became human, He became part of our priesthood and, as God, He became an eternally sustaining priesthood embodied in human form.

In reality, Melchizedek is humanity in its pristine, eternal, divine intent. We cannot become more than what we were in the mind of God, so if we are to become what we are, we must return to what we are in the mind of God. Melchizedek was the original process in the mind of God that manifested in humanity and then in God becoming human and entering into that. So God became us in order for He Himself to be initiated into our own order that He gave us through the Order of Melchizedek. This is the order that the Holy One,

the Eternal One, the Most High God, El Elyon, the glorious and majestic One, intended for human beings. It is a human order, though eternal, and it can only function effectively with human beings who have accessed their eternal nature, their immortal nature, and the light that is within them.

Jesus Christ, Our Lord, calls himself the Light of the World, and Melchizedek represents the light that directs creation, pointing the way to the human destiny, illuminating the scrolls of the human life structure according to the pattern of God. God became human and initiated Himself into our order, the Melchizedek Order, the "My King is Righteousness Order," the "My King is Peace Order," which is also the "Order of Sonship." The whole pattern between sonship and priesthood is clear. This is the order that God intended for humanity, and into which God Himself desires to be initiated. It is why He became human. Since this is the pattern and God's intent, it continues to be replicated through us. We are not the High Priest, yet we are priests after the Order of Melchizedek. And this priesthood, like the priesthood of Aaron, can only be inherited or entered into through initiation.

So let us clarify the levels. You have inherited the lineage of the Melchizedek principle and carry the genetic principle through your new birth from heaven. When you are born from above through the spirit and the water, the gene gets activated. However, then you must consciously be initiated into that. This is what the writer of Hebrews was complaining about when he says we are immature.[13] He was essentially saying, "Look, you have been born with this genetic 'my-king-is-righteousness' gene" similar to Noah. By the way, that is what made Noah perfect in his generation. The Melchizedek gene that is in you is born with you in your new birth.

13   Hebrews 5:11-14

But there has to be an initiation, a kind of spiritual technological movement, whereby you become conscious of your embeddedness and connection to this eternal priesthood. Many people are born into priesthoods, but they do not ever become conscious of it.

How did Jesus gain this in His own time? We do not have to go through what Jesus went through because He did it for us. We may need to endure many things, but we do not pay for our salvation; it is already done. Our birth in the Melchizedek principle is real. However, to raise that consciousness, there are Melchizedek technologies that we must access. We have talked a little bit about that — the bread and wine, for example, that Jesus brought back into play in creation, which is meant to raise our consciousness to the level of El Elyon's vibration and to vibrate in alignment with the sequence, frequency, and cadence of the mind of God.

Communion is more than just the bread and the wine. It is a form of fellowship through which we offer each other our essence in worship. This raises our consciousness beyond what the writer of Hebrews called "primary things" to a higher level. In this way, we embody the mystery that God intended. And we do this through communion, which is not limited to just the bread and wine. Fellowship and love for one another, as well as our conversations, allow us to become a sustaining principle for each other during struggles. Just like the old churches used to say, we become Christ for one another and become the Body of Christ, nourishing and sustaining each other.

We will come back and talk more about Melchizedek, but it seems that you and I are Melchizedek, and Christ, our Lord, was initiated into our humanity in order to become our High Priest in that order. He needed to become sinless

and become one of us so that we could be returned to the original sinless position of Melchizedek in the mind of God. This is not achieved through our own righteousness but through the giving of God. When God joins himself to our order, it becomes divine.

Can you imagine God coming to your house and saying, "Okay, I am now a member of your family. am joining myself to this DNA"? The DNA would change and that is exactly what happened. The whole process of the coming of the Son and the incarnation of Christ is for God to become a member of the order of humanity. This order is made by His Son to return humanity to its pristine position in the mind of God before creation. He came to make us an eternal priesthood, continuously serving before the Lord, no longer offering sacrifices of blood, but offering sacrifices of fellowship, worship, faith, and love, allowing new worlds to emerge. It allows us to stand at the edge of nothingness and bring into reality what was in the mind of God. Blessed be the name of the Lord! Glory be to Him who was, is, and ever shall be!

We are going to look at all the aspects of the Melchizedek Order and I will say some controversial things along the way. This Melchizedek Priesthood becomes an embodiment of all the things that the earthly priesthood was supposed to manifest, without its imperfections and without the need for blood sacrifice. I still do not understand why Christians want to talk about offering blood sacrifices in the temple, when Melchizedek met Abraham, he did not offer any sacrifice, and Abraham offered no blood sacrifice. Blood sacrifice is not a part of the principle of Melchizedek. The blood sacrifice was necessary for sustaining creation before the Messiah came. However, once the Messiah became part of the human genome, the human genetic process, and a member according to the Order of Humanity, then humanity did not need the sacrifice any longer. It needs only to participate in the complete sacrifice that was made. So, what does this priesthood do? It takes us back to a time before there was any brokenness in creation, before there was any failure on the part of humanity, even before physical man was made in creation and a body was given in order to infuse the body back into its immortal context — in other words, *your* immortality of the body.

Chapter 2

THE MELCHIZEDEK CONSCIOUSNESS

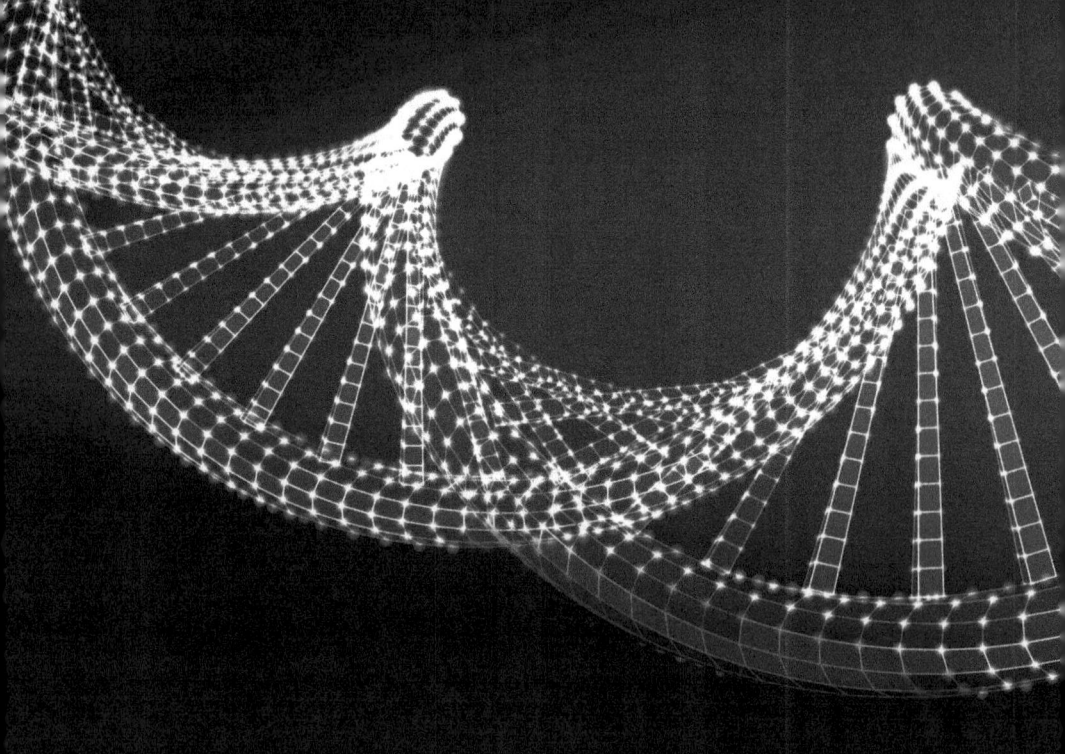

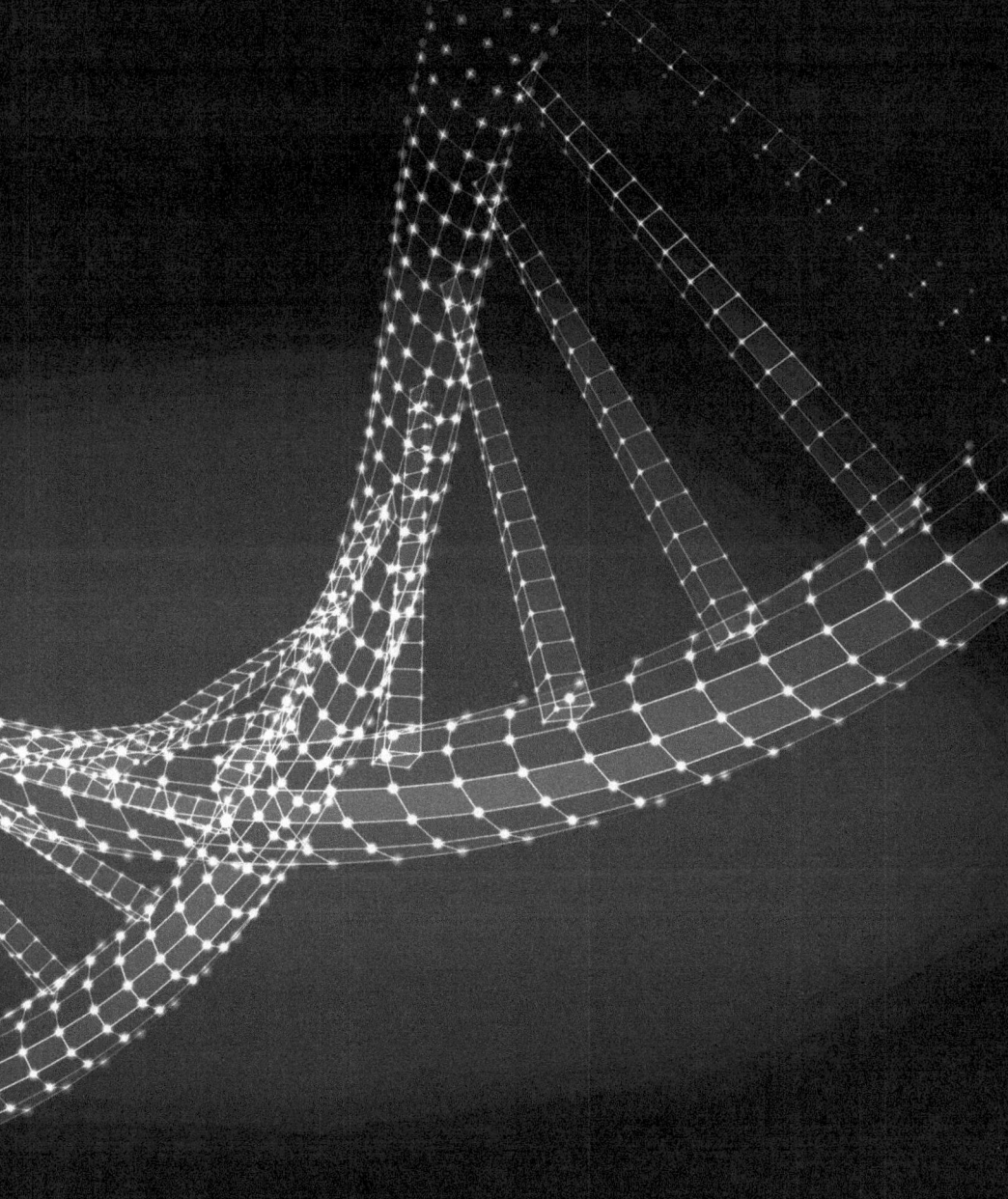

It is sometimes easy for people like me to forget that, even being Hebrew, God is the God of the whole world, not just the God of the Hebrews. The Lord constantly reminds us, "I am the Lord your God," but we know that He is the God of the entire universe.

For the earth is the Lord's, and all it contains. (1 Corinthians 10:26)

God's original intent for humanity is to participate in the fullness of who God is and, once created and established, humanity will continue for all eternity to reign, rule, and enjoy the fullness of who God is for them.

We refer to the "great mutual exchange," which is an alchemical process. Here is how it works: In the mind of God, man existed. Let us call that man the Melchizedek thought, intent, and framework. So Melchizedek is the original intent, thought, and framework for humanity, and also the framework for any legitimate priesthood that arises in creation. All true and authentic priesthood must arise from this authentic, divine frame. I have told you already that this Melchizedek principle is the original, divine intent for man. In a sense, Melchizedek is the pre-creation Adam in the mind of God — what my students would know as "Adam Kadmon." You need to be in my other classes to fully understand this concept. This principle of Melchizedek has two aspects to it. Remember the Bible says that Melchizedek is the king of peace. All of Melchizedek's characteristics are reflections of God's inner being. You get the point.

Look at it this way. if God is eternal, the projective process of God's mind says that Melchizedek must be eternal or have the potential of being reinserted into eternity. That is one aspect. The second aspect is if God *is* righteousness (not just if God is righteous), Melchizedek must be righteous or have the possibility of being made righteous as God is righteous. In other words, God's thoughts projected everything that He is within His being towards Melchizedek so that, whether Melchizedek is in the realm of ideas, which is only in the mind of God, or in the realm of manifestation, which is

anything that God is, Melchizedek is or has the potential to become.

The Melchizedek principle of that being in the mind of God is important to understand. I just said a word that may be new to you, but the Spirit will speak to you at a deeper level, not just through your ears, but with the Spirit of God. You have the Spirit of God, so you will hear this at a deeper level, not just with your religious background or church understanding, but with your spirit. An intuitive divine principle has been activated in you by being born from above, which means you understand more mysteries than you think. You have a lot in you. Your genetic structure, being born from heaven, means you know heaven more than you can explain. And you even know God more than you can talk about. You know who you are more than you can manifest at the present moment. So, do not run away from a mystery just because it does not make sense in your current understanding.

When we started teaching about being born from above and saying that a human being must be born of the Spirit, people got discombobulated and angry and rejected the idea without thinking. I was trying to show believers how unique they are in the world, but it would have been easier for me to tell them, "You're terrible; you have nothing to offer God; you're just like everyone else," It would have been easier for me to make them feel bad about themselves, guilty about things they have never done, and force them to try to heal the wound of Adam that has already been healed by Jesus Christ. That would have made people happy and convicted, but teaching something that makes people happy, hopeful, and motivated to reach their full potential tends to make people angry for some reason.

Let us now come back to the realm of manifestation. This Melchizedek, who is man in his pristine perfection within the mind of God, was projected by God to be the being that officiated the death of the Lamb before the foundation of the world. He is also the pattern by which Adam was created, but this Melchizedek in the time of spiraling in the process is a projection of the Son within the Godhead. Pay attention to this — he is the Son within the Godhead. This means that, while the principle of Melchizedek is a projected humanity, it is a projected humanity of the manifestation of sonship internal to the Godhead as well. Do you understand? The Melchizedek principle, then, while being a projection of Divinity and serving as a type, also represents the Son. You see, you do not need a priesthood inside of God; you need a priesthood to mediate creation. However, you cannot be a priest to a people with whom you do not share a genetic structure.

The way that God created Adam in creation was by looking at the Son. The way God framed Melchizedek was by looking at the Son. So, the first Adam, or rather, Adam Kadmon (the first archetypal Adam), is the one who stood and offered the sacrifice. God looked at that being, which is a human being, as a full manifestation of the interior sonship that is in God.

You cannot separate, "Thou art a son, this day I have begotten thee"[14] from "verily, thou art a priest after the Order of Melchizedek."[15] It is a combination of both. The projection of Melchizedek as a being is the projection of sonship into creation. Let me emphasize again that God projected a human being. You could not have a Melchizedek if you did not have a Son in the Godhead. You could not have a kingship

14   Hebrews 1:5
15   Psalm 110:4; Hebrews 7:17

of righteousness or an embodiment of righteousness if it was not already present in God in the sonship of the Son.

We are not ignoring the fall of man. We know that man fell, which is the reason for the way that we now have to experience this priesthood within creation. If there was no sin, humanity would have shifted completely into this priesthood as a mediator of continuous creation, the creation of God. In other words, certain aspects of creation were truncated by the fall of man because the principle of Melchizedek was short-circuited. And the more human beings continued to fall into idolatry, the more the Melchizedek genetic frequency was subsumed and dampened so that man could not rule the universe.

Do you see the point? So, when man fell, he lost his sonship, and the image and likeness that were part of what God had in mind when He thought about the Melchizedek Order for humanity. As a result, Melchizedek could come into creation and be manifested, but he could never stay in creation because humanity no longer occupied that position or served as a reflection of that divine projection. Yet God still created humanity with His original intent to bear the Order of Melchizedek. I had a vision of Melchizedek and saw multiple projections and manifestations of Melchizedek in different cultures within creation. However, the manifestations were never permanent and perfect. The priests participated in it, but because the human body had not been redeemed and had not yet come into alignment, the original DNA had not been activated. It was submerged by idolatry.

The Melchizedek manifestations in different tribes, families, and people could not be permanent. So now we can understand more clearly the need for the "great exchange" — that is, the great exchange the Son of God within the

Godhead, who was the Lamb slain before the foundation of the world, has to take on the human body.

Melchizedek represents for us the great possibility of divine exchange because human beings were created from the position of being priests. God took the human person and the human body, and in so doing, two things happened: He became us and He restored to us the position of Melchizedek Priesthood. Without sonship, the Melchizedek Order cannot work.

What exactly was the exchange? God exchanged His eternal, spiritual structure without a body to become a body so that the genetic structure could be activated in us, and we gave Him our genes. We really did! We gave Him the human genes, and then He gave us His sonship, bringing us to completion. In this way, He was initiated into our priesthood and we were initiated into His sonship. It was an incredible exchange! He gave us His divinity, and we gave Him our position as a priest of God. It is true. He opened this reality for us, and He was initiated into our order. Remember, the Bible says that the callings of God are irrevocable (Romans 11:29), so God is not going to take away the priesthood of humanity. It is still our position. Therefore, Christ was able to take on the priesthood of humanity by becoming one of us. Do not forget that. Sonship is one of the hallmarks of the Melchizedek Priesthood. So, as He is a Son, we become sons and, as a result, we share in this incredible exchange.

Melchizedek Priesthood, transmutation, and transformation are other elements of the exchange. Since the Melchizedek Priesthood is a priesthood of righteousness, only the righteous can get into it. And since we cannot make ourselves righteous, there was an exchange of our sinful nature for His righteous nature so that we could be reinserted.

Again, this could not happen unless Christ became our High Priest. And in becoming our High Priest after the Order of Melchizedek, He now exchanges His righteousness with our righteousness, which is not righteousness at all, right? So, there is this great exchange of our deteriorating nature with His eternal sonship and His eternal righteousness. The Bible states it this way: "He who knew no sin became sin for us, that we might become the righteousness of God in Him" (2 Corinthians 5:21). That's why it says Noah was the only one found righteous in his genes.[16] For that to happen, He had to exchange His own genetic structure to activate the original genetic structure of Melchizedek through our new birth and to exchange our own unrighteousness for His righteousness. In other words, we now participate within the framework of Melchizedek-righteousness.

Here is another thing to consider. When God chose Aaron, God never made an oath. The Bible never tells us that God says, "I swear the Levitical priesthood is a priesthood forever and ever." It does say the fire on the altar shall never go out (Leviticus 6:13). But if the sacrifice has gone, why do we serve at the altar? The Messiah is not from the Levitical priesthood according to the scriptures (Hebrews 5:6). What does that mean? The priesthood of Melchizedek is based on an oath. And remember, an oath is not just a word spoken by a person. An oath is the giving of the person himself. So, to sustain the Melchizedek Priesthood, God had to give Himself — both His word and His being.

God's word is immutable and can never change. Likewise, His nature can never change. Therefore, God gave both His word and His being to re-establish and reinsert humanity into the priesthood of Melchizedek so that it would be grounded in the original, unchangeable nature of God and

16   Genesis 6:9

in the word of God that cannot pass away. For the scripture says, "Heaven and earth shall pass away but the Word of the Lord shall remain."[17] And it also says, "The grass fades, the flowers fade, but the Word of the Lord abides forever."[18]

Abraham really began to reign as a king among the Canaanites. They even said to him, "You are as a prince among us" (Genesis 23:6) because of his earlier initiation. What does it mean to be a king? Literally, it means to have dominion, authority, and a space for acting. Kings have the provision to take care of their people. Kings also bring healing to the people and the land because in ancient times a king was also a priest.

The priesthood of Melchizedek is holistic in nature. We can examine Jesus' activities to see how this works. Did you know that every time Jesus had a need, the universe provided for it? The universe bent towards Him. The Melchizedek Priesthood is in harmony with creation because the frequency of that genetic structure has an intrinsic interconnection with the original intent of God in creation, even in its fallen state. When that frequency of the priest rises to its proper level, nature and creation bend towards that priesthood to provide what it needs. It is a principle of a priesthood based on God's providence and provision--a provisional capacity inserted in creation that flows from the realm of heaven. It has access, even in a fallen world, to what creation has to offer, to what has been dampened in creation by the fall of man and humanity's movement away from Divinity and into idolatry.

The Melchizedek Priesthood is about carrying the manifestation of the Divine. It is a heavenly priesthood

17   Matthew 24:25; Mark 13:31; Luke 21:33
18   1 Peter 1:24-25

whereby the believer who is in it can draw from every dimensional structure of creation to bring provision to the earth in the context of their worship and service to God. This is an initiation into the overflowing provisional capacity of God before Whom the Melchizedek priest serves, or rather, before whom the priest serves in the Order of Melchizedek. Kingship, sonship, and being a carrier of provision are all part of this initiation.

Why did Abraham pay tithe? He paid tithes to open up the gates, or the womb of creation, so that all God intended could manifest in Abraham's life. By the end of his life, it was said, "And God blessed Abraham with everything"[19] (HaShem berak Abraham bakkol).

It is true that Abraham had been able to make things happen before, but by the time he had finished being initiated, the Bible says that God blessed Abraham with everything, with all things. This means that all of creation was bent towards Abraham to make sure that the divine provision for his kingship and position on earth was not dependent on the Canaanites. Notice that when Sarah died and they offered to give him the place for free, he said, "No." He said, "No, for I will pay for it."[20] If he was not operating in the priesthood of Melchizedek, he would have been at the mercy of these unbelievers, and if they had given him all of that for free, he would have ended up being their servant. But he paid for it, thereby operating as the priest of Melchizedek. And this is part of what God meant when He spoke to Israel about who they were going to be and how He would bless their bread and their water. In a sense, He said He would bless their bread and wine, which is the principle for accessing

19 Genesis 24:1 וַיהוָה בֵּרַךְ אֶת־אַבְרָהָם בַּכֹּל
20 Genesis 23:12-13

divine provision by entering and stepping into the realm of the Father and receiving from there.

To operate in this way, those in the Kingdom still need to understand and activate this principle. The genetic structure must be activated so that whoever carries the possibility of turning the sacramental principle of the universe into a provisional principle in every context will find they can actually do this. And by the way, Jesus was speaking of this when He said, "I came that they might have life and have it more abundantly"[21] He said, "I am the door; if anyone enters through Me, he will be saved, and will go in and out and find pasture."[22] All of this was part of the Melchizedek lineage and process. So, if a believer begins to operate accordingly and becomes a gateway of divine providence and provision, then God allows creation to bend towards them. They become a door of hope in the valley of suffering, a door of provision in the valley of lack, a door of mercy in the valley of violence and vengeance, a door of grace in the valley of condemnation and guilt, and a door of love.

To return to the book of Hebrews, we cannot discuss it without talking about who Jesus Christ is. Remember, He never called the angels His sons, and He never said to them, "You are My Son. Sit on My right hand until I make your enemies your footstool."[23] This is a Melchizedek process. The reason you and I can say we are seated in heavenly places and the satans, serpents, adders, and scorpions are under our feet is because we participate in the Melchizedek Priesthood. And it is through participating in and being initiated into the Melchizedek Priesthood that Jesus Christ earned the right to have all things under His feet. The book of Psalms says,

---

21 John 10:10
22 John 10:9
23 Hebrews 1:13

"You have placed all things under His feet."[24] This promise is only possible for those who fully participate in the Order of Melchizedek. While humanity can work to overcome certain things, the full manifestation of it is only for those who have been born with that genetic structure, initiated into that consciousness, and become an embodiment of that righteousness. It is an incredible process.

The renewal of youth is another aspect of the Melchizedek principle. Melchizedek is an original divine projection of Divinity who carries the fullness of God without death and has never been subject to death. This image has never been subject to death because it represents man as being directly descended from God, not just a man born of a woman. This immortality can be found only through the new birth. When a person becomes a direct descendant of God, the principle of death cannot reign over them. Jesus said, "He that believes in Me shall never die and if he were dead, yet shall he live again"[25] at the tomb of Lazarus when He resurrected Lazarus.

This was an activation of the principle of immortality that God originally intended for humanity. At the point of Jesus' initiation into the human Order of Melchizedek, He exchanged that original intent with its temporal and unoriginal manifestation of that intent so that He overcame death in us. He overcame corruption in our mortal bodies by releasing His Spirit and Himself.

The story of Noah and the son of Nir[26] sounds similar because they were all born in different ways. In the case of Noah, he was born through his mother and father. In the case of the son of Nir, he was born from an old woman who

24 Psalm 8:6
25 John 11:25-26
26 2 Enoch 71

could never get pregnant and the husband never knew her. These stories point to the fact that in our new birth, we have the mark of the priesthood emblazoned in our hearts and being, which is how we participate in the narrative of the Melchizedek Priesthood principle. It is also about those who were not born of natural flesh or the will of man. That is what John chapter 3 describes when Jesus tells Nicodemus that he must be born again. It is about the Melchizedek birth process. And it is about those who were not born according to the will of man or the pattern of the flesh but were born according to God.

Then why did the Word become flesh (John 1)? Becoming flesh enabled the Word to bring human flesh, the human body, into that priesthood, removing it from its fallen nature so that it can embody (or manifest) the Melchizedek nature. I said earlier that this is the mystery of kingship, the mystery of sonship, the mystery of creation, and the pattern of creation. So, without the priesthood of Melchizedek, navigating and officiating at the original pre-foundation altar where the Lamb was willing to give His life, there would be no creation. By the activity of the Melchizedek Priesthood, creation is framed and manifested. Creation would still be in the realm of non-manifestation if humanity was not projected back and forth from the mind of God into the context of the original foundation. Creation would still be in the realm of possibility, not in the realm of reality if I can put it that way. In the same way, the salvation of humanity would still be in the realm of possibility, not in the realm of reality if Christ did not become Melchizedek. I want to say again, He was not Melchizedek; He *became* Melchizedek. He was not human originally; He became human, and in becoming Melchizedek, He drew us back into what we were supposed to do.

Consequently, the more the Melchizedek consciousness arises, the more new technologies arise because creation gives its secrets to this being that stood at the edge of the mind of God, which God allowed to be the officiating being for the sacrifice of the Lamb before creation. The more people are initiated into this consciousness, the more strongly the Melchizedek consciousness arises. Many people are born into this, as they have been born from above. However, the majority of those born from above are not initiated because initiation requires a consciousness that has been transformed. A transfusion or transmutation of consciousness that raises it to the God-vibration is necessary for it to function as a Melchizedek frequency in creation. As you become initiated into the Melchizedek consciousness, you should expect new ideas and technologies to come to mind. Believers should lead the way in scientific, technological, business, social, and spiritual revolutions because that is what the Melchizedek consciousness is meant to inspire.

In other words, Enoch was a priest after the Order of Melchizedek, but he was not a High Priest because he was still a fallen person. However, he still accessed many technologies. Enoch, for example, was able to build flying machines that allowed him to levitate and jump from one galaxy to another. He went through all kinds of worlds and then came to the tenth world where the inside was bigger than the outside. He was able to lift this place into the heavens, not just in his imagination, but with his physical body.[27] The technology that Enoch developed is yet to be replicated in this world. Jesus ascended into heaven, and Elijah did too, but Elijah needed a chariot to take him. When the human body itself becomes the chariot of God, it can move trans-dimensionally, trans-terrestrially, and trans-celestially in different dimensions of space and the

27 The First Book of Enoch

heavens. It can go in and out of the throne room and meet with the Father God. Right now, we can move spiritually and our souls can go up, but a technology is coming by virtue of the human activation of the Melchizedek principle that transcends nations. And, by the way, the idea of "no Gentile and no Greek" is a Melchizedek principle because, as we have seen, it is a human principle. Every human being is initiated. The idea of "no male or female" is a Melchizedek principle because Melchizedek existed before Adam was separated into male and female. It is for everyone.

It is amazing what God does within such paradigms. Creation responds and gives up its hidden histories and secrets, but it must be given to those who are conscious, not just at the level of ordinary daily religious rituals. It is given to those who are conscious at the frequency of God, or at the God-frequency level. That is what Melchizedek is supposed to be.

When someone attains this God-frequency, not only does creation respond, but it allows other new creation ideas to manifest within it. You are participating with the Melchizedekians, if I may coin a word in this convergence, which is an exchange of your sin for His righteousness, your limitations for His limitlessness, and your "something-that-is-nothing" with His "nothing-that-is-everything." You enter in by His grace, by His grace, by His grace, by His grace, and His mercy. We are initiated into the mystery of life, which is not life as we know it, but the embedded immortality of the original divine intent within human beings.

Remember, these things were inserted into human beings: the resurrection principle and the perpetual regeneration of the human being without intermediary through direct influence, direct engagement, and direct face-to-face encounter with the Holy One. This is the light that we are meant to become. These things were given so that we can have life, as the Master said, and have it more abundantly. The idea of the mystery of life is carried by the Melchizedek principle. By conjoining Himself to us and participating in our humanity, He brought back into our being, through His divinity, the mystery of life, which is immortality cloaked in light.

This conjunction with the Melchizedek principle allowed the body of Jesus Christ to come out of the grave. As a physical body, He became our High Priest and embodied Melchizedek. Now we draw from His being, not as fallen beings but as risen beings. Do not forget that when He died, we died too. When He suffered, we also suffered. When He was buried, we were buried with Him. And when He rose, we rose with Him. He ascended to the heavenly places and we too are seated there with Him. Just like He feels all things, we also feel everything. We are just not conscious of it yet. If you say that you are in Christ and where He is, then you are there with Him. In John 14:3, He said, "Where I am, you may be also." This means that you are now with Him everywhere. Even though you are localized in one place, you are non-local, and you are in every place at the same time.

This is because of the conjunction, the joining of the Son of God into our order. Again, He is a member of our order and has been raised to be our High Priest because He shares our nature and our life. He has exchanged everything that we were and brought us back to what we were originally supposed to be. The principle of life has been activated in us so we are alive. If we are alive, then the Melchizedek principle was not a death-producing thing in our sense of death. It was not a corruption-creating priesthood where

you killed something, burned it, threw it away, and part of it rotted. It was the sacrifice of life unto life.

The process by which Melchizedek operated was to release life that gives life, not life that leads to death. It was the principle of Melchizedek operating in the garden that allowed Adam to lead a perpetually renewed life. And everyone who has ever been redeemed had to have that Melchizedek principle activated since Christ joined Himself to our order that God the Father, the Son, and the Holy Spirit intended for us, which has been made a reality for us again through Jesus Christ our Lord. It is by faith in Him that we stand here today, like the lame man. It is by faith in the name of Jesus Christ that this man stands here today, completely made whole. Finally, it is by faith in Christ and His conjunction with us as the Melchizedek being and His participation in our order that we stand here today, ready to manifest immortality and light and ready to have a transmuted body that is able to self-replicate across time. It is all in Christ.

Like everything else, there are levels of initiation which God puts us through to raise our consciousness. Some of the trials we go through test whether we are able to cross that threshold and enter into the new level. We sometimes fail to move to that level because we are satisfied with a limited consciousness rather than one that has been expanded to the level of Divinity. This means that we have to sacrifice what we hold dear in terms of our religious beliefs and other things in order to move to that level. Therefore, there has to be a constant reinsertion and self-submission, entering into the suffering of Christ, and entering into the life of Christ. It is a redemptive consciousness. Redemption is real. There is no human being that cannot be redeemed. There is nothing in framed, physical creation that cannot be redeemed. It is different when you begin to talk about spiritual things or things that exist in the ethereal realm. But we keep moving towards the mark of our high calling in Christ, which is the mark of becoming fully Melchizedek, or becoming full Melchizedek priests, lacking nothing in the arena of our priesthood with God.

My encounter with the being I came to know as Melchizedek changed the way I view believers and the way I talk to them. Sometimes I am harsh because I know that believers do not know who they are, but I try not to be harsh all the time. Part of our issue is that we want to maintain natural constructs as a way of carrying out the Melchizedek Priesthood, but most of the time our so-called natural constructs are actually constructs of the fallen nature of man.

Do you see how far removed the church is from the Melchizedek Order in terms of what it is supposed to do? The first manifestation of this is the level of division we fight with, which has nothing to do with who Jesus Christ is or the redemption of man, but just with our ideology and patterns. And Christians are some of the first to run to it. I am also guilty of that, especially with my Hebrew background. But we must move beyond taking our natural construct as the basis of our priesthood and move towards supernatural, hyper-natural non-natural, and divine constructs as the basis of our relationship with one another.

Melchizedek Priesthood

The more we make divisions based on the structures of humanity and its fallen nature, the less we experience the Melchizedek movement. What strikes me is that, in the Bible, Melchizedek, as he was manifested in Salem, was a Canaanite priest, yet he reached out to Abraham, who was a Hebrew, and did not turn away from him. Isn't that interesting? This means Melchizedek already saw the possibility of the unity of all humanity. The funny thing is, we keep fighting against humanity becoming one. We say we want to become one, and yet we continuously fight about how different we are. This entire evangelical construct is confusing and contradictory when you think about it. One time we say we are all one human being and then turn around and say we do not want human beings to be one. We want to maintain cultural, tribal, and national boundaries, while we are talking about the unity of humanity. It does not make any sense.

We must move beyond this construct we have created. Yes, it is true, God imposed it, but our division is a punishment from God, not a gift from God. It was a curse from God. But now, Christ has come so that the Melchizedek principle being made manifest means that there is neither Jew nor Gentile, neither Indian nor African, neither Malaysian nor Singaporean, neither American nor Russian, or neither Australian nor New Zealander when it comes to faith. The problem is that we take so much pride in our differences that we do not take pride in what God has actually created in us by giving us a genetic, inter-relational structure that is not bound by the curse that God put upon the people in the Bible.

It is hard to say what we believe as Christians, and yet still make the same mistakes. God has been dealing with me on this, especially given my Hebrew background. I need to start asking, "Which is more important — the Melchizedek Order or my Levitical Order?" My Levitical Order gives me understanding and many other things, but the Melchizedek Order wipes out the divisions among humanity. It is meant to remove the demarcation that has made us enemies with one another. The Melchizedek Order is the answer that will bring peace to the world. Tribal priesthood will not achieve this. It is a global priesthood and the priesthood of all humanity who believes, that will wipe out the demarcations and make us one. It will bring us back into the full priesthood where creation responds to us according to our Father's original intent.

This has happened through our Lord Jesus Christ, our Savior, our Redeemer, who offers this to all of humanity. He does not just offer it to one side; He offers it to all of us. If you believe and trust in Him, if this gene is born in you, and if you have been initiated, then you ought to be in movement towards peace.

Chapter 3

THE SACRIFICE
OF MELCHIZEDEK

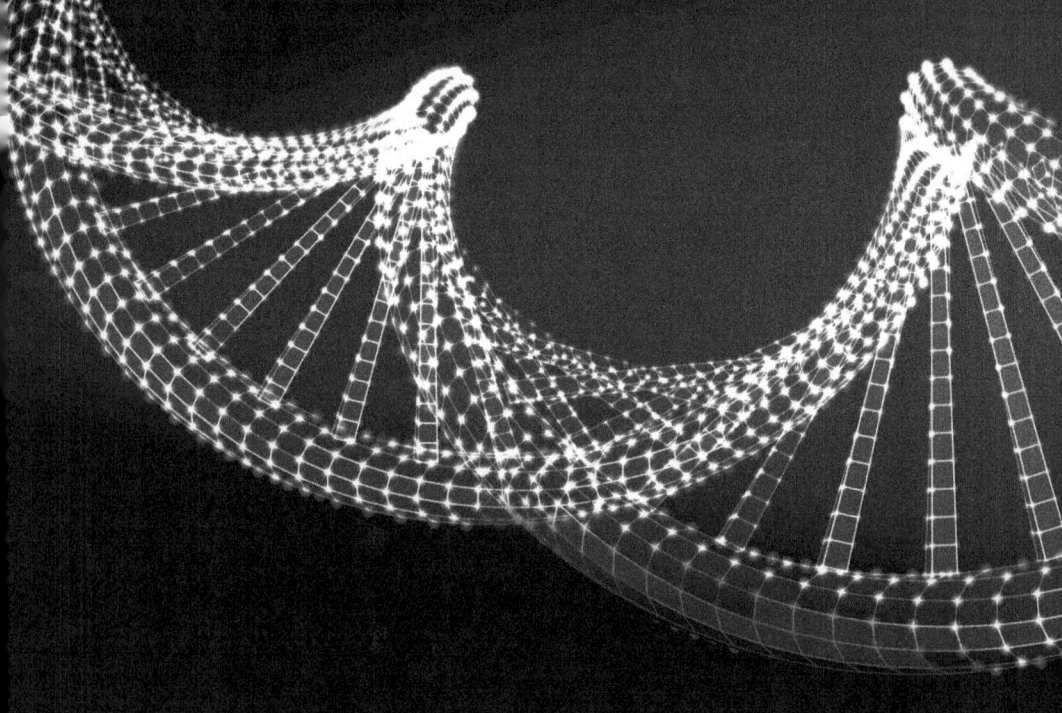

The Priesthood of Melchizedek, according to the Bible, is the only priesthood in the world in which the High Priest is higher than the heavens.[28] Its locative dimension is exactly the point from which God reigns. We call it a heavenly priesthood, or alternatively, the throne room priesthood, because only God, whose throne is above the heavens, is higher than the heavens. We minister from the heavenly dimensions, and by that we mean that it is a multi-dimensional priesthood. It does not just minister in one dimension because the Person who has taken on the High Priest position is present everywhere God's presence is accepted and believed in. It is a once-and-for-all complete and total sacrifice that is offered only once and is not offered by the priests.[29] Humanity is the priest that offered the sacrifice, but the sacrifice itself is not given daily. It is a once-and-for-all permanent sacrifice, which means that once you come into this, there is no more sacrificial system. It does not mean there is no more cost for your life, for giving, or for entering; it just means there are no more sacrificial systems.

---

28 Hebrews 7:25
29 Hebrews 9:23-28

We need to revisit this again what I said earlier. If you are part of the Melchizedek Priesthood and have accepted it and come from the nations, why do you need sacrifices to continue in the temple? You do not need the sacrificial system any longer. Let us get back to the main point. It is a once-and-for-all, eternal sacrifice. It is a temporary sacrifice that connects to an eternal sacrifice. There was only one sacrifice made to create the world, so there was only one sacrifice to redeem the world. There are many sacrifices needed to cover sins and help humanity thrive or survive, but there is only one sacrifice made for creation and one sacrifice made for redemption.

The sacrifice of creation is a sacrifice of life from the life of the Son of God. The sacrifice of redemption is a sacrifice of life, from death to life, of the Son of God. It is always a sacrifice by the Son moving towards life. The Melchizedek principle requires a once-and-for-all sacrifice for whatever it does. Therefore, you cannot make one sacrifice for the redemption of the world and then make specific sacrifices for a specific group of people. It is a one-size-fits-all sacrifice.

It is not a sacrifice for the failure of the High Priests because the Melchizedek High Priest never failed. Thus, the original archetype remains unsullied. This is what Christ brought back into creation, the original image of Divinity, so that now we can become as if we have never sinned. It is the one redemptive sacrifice. It is not a sacrifice made from a position of infirmity but from a position of victory, wholeness, and power. Interestingly, in the scriptures, Christ did not tell you to sacrifice yourself because your sacrifice would not have been sufficient. You have come below the Melchizedek Order. A created being could not serve as the perfect sacrifice. The purpose of the Melchizedek Priesthood is to return humanity to the perfection of Divinity and the original intent of God.

If you made this sacrifice from a human perspective, you would only return to a human position. But if God did it by becoming a part of you, then He can return you to His original intention. That is why Christ became human. What is the key point? We have a High Priest who sits at the right hand of the throne of majesty in heaven. This priesthood sits in a place of power, which we can call the place of majesty. It is a majestic priesthood, and it is located at the right hand of the throne of majesty in the heavens. In every heavenly dimension, the place of power is reserved for a Melchizedek priest. This means that in all of creation, both what has already been created and what is still being manifested, needs a Melchizedek Priesthood to sit in the right-hand place, the place of power, in order for it to manifest the full original intent of God.

Christ sits at the right hand of the Father Almighty, the right hand of power. This text is very clear that this High Priest sits at the right hand of the majesty in the heavens. In one place it says that he is made higher than all the heavens. So, how does this High Priest sit on the right hand of majesty in the heavens? Not just in *heaven*, but in the *heavens* (plural)? Who sits there as a manifestation of the High Priest? You do, because the High Priest is man becoming God, or man who is God. As we discussed previously, it is for all believers to sit on the throne of power, and only those who participate in this Melchizedek Principle can do that. The right hand of the throne of the majesty in heaven refers to the place of power, the place of beauty, the place of the glory, and the authority of God. So, Melchizedek priests, whom you are, serving under the High Priest, sit in those places in all the dimensions of heaven.

In addition, this High Priest ministers in the sanctuary of the true tabernacle, which the Lord pitched, not man. I am not speaking of a ministration in a tabernacle that can be removed. A person who is a priest in the Order of Melchizedek serves at the temple not made with hands (Hebrews 9:11). The scripture says, "a minister in the sanctuary and in the true tabernacle, which the Lord set up, not man."[30] What does that mean? This person serves in the tabernacle in heaven because that is the tent not made by hands. Right? Are you ready for this? It means that these people minister to human beings who are the temple of the whole of God because it is the temple not made by human hands but made by the hand of God. There are two temples—one that is above and one that is below. The temple above is in the heavens, as mentioned in Revelation 18. The second one is a man who as a priest is also a temple. So, we minister within the construct of the temple of our being.

You can call it the temple of the human soul, the temple of the human body, or the temple of the human being. These are not made by human hands, and for the believer, even right now, we minister to our bodies and to other human beings who are also temples not made with human hands. The ultimate human temple is the temple of Christ since He is the uniquely positioned tabernacle of God within creation. Creation was not made by hands but by the Word of God's mouth. Similarly, Christ's body was not made by human construction, but by the Word of God. And your body that will become immortal is a result of the Logos, the Word of God, which constructs it and makes it like God's essence. It becomes the body of God that He manifests through His being.

30 Hebrews 8:2

So the Bible speaks of the body of creation represented through man, the temple below, and the tabernacle that is above. The earthly tabernacle is fully represented by the Person of Christ. Let me address some religious spirits who might hear this in the future and get upset. The body of Christ is the temple of God, and we worship that body. For when He sent the Son into the world, what did He say? Let the angels worship Him. And here is a mystery that is amazing to me: Christ took on a human body, and we see Him, though we do not know Him as a natural person anymore. Yet He took the human body, a glorified body, and we worship that body. Christ serves at a temple of His own body and as the High Priest of His own body. And we serve as priests to that body because He Himself is that pure tabernacle.

And that is where the Melchizedek Order is different. "Every High Priest is appointed to offer both gifts and sacrifices."[31] Therefore, it is necessary that the High Priest also has something to offer.

What does our High Priest offer? Himself. And in the process, we offer ourselves together with Him. And in this offering, we do not offer ourselves as a sacrifice; we offer ourselves as a gift. He offered Himself as a sacrifice, but now He comes with us, and we offer ourselves as gifts in the process of that sacrifice so we can draw from the sacrifice and receive its benefits. Whatever He has paid for, we are the beneficiaries because He brings us as a gift to the temple before the Father, which is Himself. When He stands before God, you are standing before God; when He looks at the Father, you are looking at the Father; when He speaks to the Father, you are speaking to the Father. You are participating in His High Priesthood. This is not like the Levitical priesthood where there is so much separation.

31 Hebrews 8:3

When the Melchizedek High Priest goes into the presence of the Father, He takes you with Him.

High Priest

Whatever He does in the presence of God is attributed to you. As you function as a Melchizedek High Priest, you participate with Christ in that. You do not stay in the second temple or in the second partition of the temple. You do not stay outside the temple. You actually go into the inner place, which is His body and His being, into the presence of the Father. This means you actually minister to the inner sanctum of God Himself.

Every High Priest was appointed to offer gifts, so it is necessary that this High Priest also offer a gift. God receives us as a gift, and Christ offers us as gifts to the Father. We are redeemed gifts. If you read Hebrews 8 again, you will see that it is talking about gifts. Not all offerings to God in the temple were sacrifices.

We focus on the sacrifice, but we forget all the gifts given to God in the temple that resulted from the atoning work. There was blood sacrifice, but there were also thank offerings. Gifts are referred to as thank offerings, peace offerings, or other things that are given. These gifts are not necessarily blood sacrifices and do not have to be blood sacrifices.

Blood sacrifice was necessary for atonement, but it was not necessary for all the other aspects of relationship between God and humanity.

When sin is removed, what is the purpose of blood sacrifice? It is a perpetual gifting for the sustenance of the life that the giver has provided. If you were in Israel or in any tribe on earth, and your family is not a lineage of priesthood, you cannot make offerings or be a priest. A priest must constantly give offerings, bring gifts, or make sacrifices before God. If Christ were on earth, even though He became a human being, He would not be able to be a priest in Israel.[32] Therefore, the location of the sacrifice had to be changed. And the locations of the offering, intercession, and gift-giving had to be changed as well. Thus, He had to serve in a different dimension, one that is different from the earth.

The passage in Hebrews 8 says, "Who served that which is a copy."[33] So, the people served a copy, but the Melchizedek Priesthood is the real thing, not a copy. When people say that the Melchizedek Priesthood is a type, they miss the point — it is the real thing. It is not a type; it is the real thing in which Christ. That is what the writer of Hebrews says:

> Now if he were on earth, he would not be a priest at all, seeing there are those who offer the gifts according to the law; who serve that which is a copy and shadow of the heavenly things, *even as Moses is warned of God when he is about to make the tabernacle: for, See, saith he, that thou make all things according to the pattern that was showed thee in the mount.*
>
> **But now hath he obtained a ministry the more excellent, by so much as he is also the mediator of a better covenant, which hath been enacted upon better promises. For if that first covenant had been**

---

32   Hebrews 8:4
33   Hebrews 8:5

faultless, then would no place have been sought for a second. For finding fault with them, he saith,

Behold, the days come, saith the Lord, That I will make a new covenant with the house of Israel and with the house of Judah; Not according to the covenant that I made with their fathers In the day that I took them by the hand to lead them forth out of the land of Egypt;

For they continued not in my covenant, And I regarded them not, saith the Lord. For this is the covenant that I will make with the house of Israel After those days, saith the Lord;

I will put my laws into their mind, And on their heart also will I write them: And I will be to them a God, And they shall be to me a people: And they shall not teach every man his fellow-citizen, And every man his brother, saying, Know the Lord: For all shall know me, From the least to the greatest of them. For I will be merciful to their iniquities, And their sins will I remember no more. (Hebrews 8:4-12 [ASV])

This New Covenant says that He has already made an old one. What we call the Old Covenant on earth was actually a New Covenant that God made in order to sustain human beings at the time it was made. So, the New Covenant that we have is actually the oldest covenant, which was made at the time Melchizedek was projected out of the mind of God. Then Christ brought it back into creation to manifest who He is and be a part of us.

While we call our covenant a New Covenant, it is new to us because we are sold into sin, but it is an Old Covenant to

God because it is an eternal covenant that God made with Himself before even making Adam or creating the world because that covenant is eternal and as ancient as the Ancient One. It is new to us because we fell, and we are coming back to it. It is a New Covenant in light of the covenant that God made with Moses and the Israelites in the wilderness. According to the book of Hebrews, that covenant, though being made by God, is sustained only by the coming of the Messiah. Consequently, any interpretation that removes the Messiah from being the fulfillment of the original priestly covenant of God is not a good interpretation of scripture.

The priesthood of Melchizedek is a priesthood of light and it speaks light. It carries the frequency of light and manifests light. It sustains the world by light. It is a frequency of light that overcomes darkness, that causes the expansiveness of light so that darkness is constantly and completely being overcome by it. I am talking about darkness as an evil principle, but also the opening of the mysteries of God in the area of what may be considered natural darkness. I, for one, think that we are having all these breakthroughs going into different worlds because the Melchizedek frequencies are in creation by the sons of God whose Melchizedek genes are being activated in creation. Therefore, creation is responding by opening up its mysteries and allowing humanity to enter into different dimensions than we have ever entered before.

Before, we all saw these mysteries primarily in visions and trances, but now they are becoming reality that human beings are experiencing in real-time and in nature. We are entering in, activating, and accessing the Melchizedek principle at a higher level than it has ever been since Adam fell, since Enoch's time, and since the time of the rise of certain spiritual people in creation. It never vanishes. We said before that the Melchizedek principle carries the mystery of redemption, which is about humanity and creation. No matter what anybody says, when people start to supersede the scriptures, you should be suspicious of them. I am sorry, but when people begin to act as if the scriptures do not matter, you should be a bit suspicious of them because the text is still important. Our revelations must be grounded in the scriptures.

We cannot talk about us superseding Christ in the sense of doing what He has already said He has completed for us. You know, if you start saying that you have superseded Christ, then that means you can die for me for my sins. You cannot die for me for my sins. You may be able to die to create something new out of your being, but you cannot die for the sins of the world that you did not create. The one who created the world must be the one to lay down his or her life for that world. You have not created a world yet that you are capable of redeeming. You will one day when the Father allows you, but it has not happened yet. So, when you try to be the redeemer of creation, you are barking up the wrong tree, although you do carry redemption. The redemption you carry is the manifestation of the redemption of Christ and Christ came to redeem the sons of humanity. We cannot overstate this case when it comes to Hebrews 2.

> **And again, I will put my trust in him. And again, Behold, I and the children whom God hath given me. Since then the children are sharers in flesh and blood, he also himself in like manner partook of the same; that through death he might bring to nought him that had the power of death, that is, the devil; and might deliver all them who through fear of death were all their lifetime subject to bondage. For verily not to angels doth he give help, but he giveth help to the seed of Abraham. (Hebrews 2:13-16 [ASV])**

This is the reason for my argument. He does not give help to the angels but gives help to the seed of Abraham. And if you see the seed of Abraham as the new humanity, then you have to come to the realization that He is not giving help to the devil. You do not have a scriptural basis for what you are saying. I know some people keep saying that I do not understand what I am talking about, but the scripture could not have stated it better:

For verily not to angels doth he give help, but he giveth help to the seed of Abraham. Wherefore it behooved him in all things to be made like unto his brethren, that he might become a merciful and faithful High Priest in things pertaining to God, to make propitiation for the sins of the people. For in that he himself hath suffered being tempted, he is able to succor them that are tempted. (Hebrews 2:16-18 [ASV])

He was made like us, not Lucifer or Satan. He was not made like demons; He was made like a human being. He is talking about us:

Wherefore, holy brethren, partakers of a heavenly calling, consider the Apostle and High Priest of our confession, even Jesus; who was faithful to him that appointed him, as also was Moses in all his house. For he hath been counted worthy of more glory than Moses, by so much as he that built the house hath more honor than the house. (Hebrews 3:1-3 [ASV])

So, what do you want the scripture to tell you? You are not the savior of demons, satans, or idols. You are supposed to be walking towards the redemption of humanity. If you want

to throw this scripture away, then throw it away, but stop saying that you are still operating as one who follows Jesus and the scripture. Make up your own stuff and be very clear.

The Melchizedek Priesthood is a priesthood of humanity that was meant to serve God, not satans. It was not meant to reach out to satans, but to serve God for the purpose of redeeming humanity. And all that was created was to help humanity. I can understand if you want to talk about the redemption of all humanity and the possibility thereof, but when you disregard scripture and go against it by saying that Satan himself will be saved, you are moving beyond the boundaries that God has set for you. Do not say there is no boundary. God himself is the one who kicked Satan out of the garden and out of heaven, and he did not do it for the purpose of redemption.

I will keep saying this, even if people get upset. People can criticize those who have studied the scripture and disagree with their interpretation. However, if you do not read the scripture in its original language, whether it be Hebrew or Greek, and do not understand the structure of the language and how it works, then your understanding of the scripture may be limited.

I will stand by the truth of the scripture. I will not compromise it for anyone or anything. The redemption of humanity is what the Melchizedek Priesthood is all about and it is not about the redemption of Satan or any other evil force. The Bible is clear on this and I will not deviate from it. But you cannot deny what is written just to make up your own systems.

Again, the Melchizedek principle is a ministry unto God. Ezekiel 40, for instance, talks about priesthood, and in doing so, there is no mention of us going to minister to Satan. Unless you are serving Satan how can you minister to him? Unless you are embracing a doctrine of demons, how can you save demons? This is what is being purveyed all over the world, making it seem as if Christ became a demon to save a demon. The implications are very serious. If the Bible had said so, then we would believe that, but the Bible says that He did not offer His sacrifice to angels. He never said to any of the angels, "You are my son, this day have I begotten you." He did not become an angel to save angels. He became human to save humanity. The Melchizedek principle is really a construct about human beings.

I will humble myself before the Lord if the Lord tells me differently, but the text does not allow me to do that. In fact, the whole experience of who Christ is does not allow me to draw the conclusion that He ministers to demons. So why did Christ make war with devils and not try to save them? Why did He come to deliver us from the hands of those who had power and kept us in bondage,[34]? The Bible uses the word "discomfited." In other words, Jesus defeated him, destroyed him and his work, and removed him. And at the end, He bound him in chains. How do we avoid all of that to talk about something that the scripture does not teach? My question to those of you who are buying into that teaching is have you actually ministered to your fellow human beings enough for you to be able to talk about saving Satan, who is your enemy? It is not just your enemy; it is a mortal enemy of humanity. Because he is your enemy, God has made him His enemy, and he hates God as much as he hates you. Stop pretending to do something that God never sent you to do. I am going to keep saying it.

34   Hebrews 2:14-16

For those of you who want to continue following that teaching, you must know that at a certain point, you are no longer following Jesus because you are going against what He did. If you can convince yourself that you have surpassed Jesus as a being, then you can convince yourself that you have surpassed God who inspired the scriptures to be written. It is not an issue of interpretation. The Bible either says it or it does not. And we use scripture to interpret scripture. We do not merely take one part of scripture; we work these things out. I do not hate you. I do not dislike you. I am not upset with you. I just think what you are teaching is full of nonsense. And that is my interpretation.

The main point is I love you and I believe in you. I believe that you will be saved, even if you have the wrong doctrine and still believe in Jesus Christ. I do not think you are saved by your doctrine, but it is misleading to teach people false doctrine. The church has examined this for two thousand years and has determined that it does not fit with the doctrine of who Christ is. We need to be careful so that we do not mislead people and prevent them from living a full, righteous life in creation by giving them false hope.

Because Melchizedek pertains to human beings, it gives you the authority to rule and have dominion. One of the things we have noticed in terms of studying Melchizedek is that the tabernacle, or Succoth, is fulfilled in Melchizedek priests. This is because the Melchizedek priests embody the actual "tabernacling" of Divinity. The real Succoth is not made by human hands; it is a tabernacle not made by human hands. Even though we admit that there will be a temple that will descend from heaven, any temple that is built by man on earth is destined to be destroyed. If the first temple, the second temple, and the temple of Herod were all destroyed, then even if we build the temple of Ezekiel with human hands and do not allow it to descend from heaven, it will still be destroyed. The cankerworms will eat it. In two thousand years, someone might need gold if the Messiah does not come completely. Someone might come to steal from the temple and destroy it to get the gold, just like the Babylonians did when they took the gold and other precious metals from the temple to further their own spiritual processes and power.

The fulfillment of the Feast of Tabernacles can be achieved only by the Melchizedek priests. The reason for the temporary "succoth" is because the permanent one is coming, and that permanent one is us. The true Succoth is those who truly know the Lord, know God and have hearts that are now tablets of divine embodiment where the handwriting of God is written on their hearts. And like the story of the Melchizedek child born to Nir and Noah, their hearts have the mark of the High Priest Melchizedek who is an embodiment of righteousness given by God.

Remember, I am not saying that if you have a wrong doctrine and do not understand certain doctrine, you will go to hell. But I think it is important to avoid misleading God's people because a false doctrine can also prevent you from fully participating in what has been provided for you. As a result, you may have to wait until the end of time or the fulfillment of time to receive what has been promised to you, since the wrong doctrine and lack of knowledge can lead to perishing, which is what the Bible says. When you give people incorrect knowledge, you are actually putting them on a path to perishing, not necessarily hell, but it manifests in their inability to fulfill their destiny as they should.

Here is something else to consider. According to my interpretation of the scripture, the bride of Christ, or the city, emerged from Him at the slaying of the Lamb. Melchizedek

Priesthood. So, when the Melchizedek Priesthood appears, everyone who participates in it rules over a city and is attached to it. This city serves as a technology for terra-formation and transmutation — a creative manifestation of God's original intent that accesses and interconnects with all dimensions, including the highest heavens. Therefore, those who teach that the heavenly Jerusalem is a manifestation of us are not entirely correct. They have made a mistake, but this mistake is not as serious as misleading people into thinking they can save the devil. The idea of the city is that we, as sons, are attached to a city (which in human language is the Bride) that carries the essence and being of the one who is sent to do the work.

Is it not amazing that a city was attached to Melchizedek and the city was called Salem? This means that when Jesus told the story of the servants with talents, he was actually talking about the embodiment of a Melchizedek principle that is always fruitful and, in the end, always reveals its own city and rulership. The city is the terra-formation technology.

I had a vision the other day that the Lamb and the Bride were working in conjunction. We call it the New Jerusalem when it comes to Earth, but it has always been there from ancient times. The New Jerusalem and the Lamb interact. In my vision, I saw a city emerging from the Lamb Who was sitting over a major city. In a flash, I saw Melchizedek slay the Lamb with his own hand. Out of the Lamb's life, which is the blood of the Lamb from the foundation, a mist rose up, framing the city. The blood of the Lamb, which is light, went into the city and refracted light. And from that refraction, there was a conjunction process before the foundation that allowed creation to be manifested.

So, there is a flow here, before the foundation of creation. There is a movement into the projected city. The Lamb, Melchizedek, and the Lamb releasing its life moved into the city and out of the 24 dimensions of the city came the process of creation. From its seven foundations, the seven days of creation emerged. From its lights came forth the 24 hours of the earth and the structures of the universe, which serve as the structure of man. Out of the pre-foundational principle and interaction, man was created to reflect the Lamb in creation as well as to become someone who can project their own city when they fulfill this principle.

So, what was Melchizedek looking for? Why did God allow him to participate? Because Melchizedek, as a human being, needed to experience what the Lamb was doing. When humanity was created, they should have been able to manifest the same thing. Everything God did was to exemplify for man what Melchizedek, as humanity, needed to do. However, since Adam fell, he was not able to manifest the city. As a result, his capacity to manifest the city was hindered. Adam lost his Melchizedek potential and could not create the city with life in it. The possibility of fulfilling the Melchizedek principle was lost.

What do we first discover about city-building in the Bible? Cain built a city from a fallen place.[35] The act of building a city was ingrained in the very foundation of the creation of the world. The city symbolizes the Bride, representing humanity as an expression of the Son of God. So, sonship produces "bridal-ship." But the human being who was meant to manifest directly from the heavenly Jerusalem did not do so. Instead, he moved away from God, which resulted in the truncation of the Melchizedek process. The city released through the blood of the Lamb was meant to be what man

---

35   Genesis 4:17

does when he becomes fully human, regardless of gender. Every time you see Melchizedek, you find him with a city or you find him manifesting something that resembles a city. For instance, the Noah's Ark was a city that could travel. When I saw this, I decided to look into it again. I discovered that Adam was supposed to remain in the garden until he could manifest his own city and become mature enough to rule. He was meant to rule the world and, with Eve, they would have reached a point where they would no longer be male and female, as Paul mentions in his writing, "Where there is neither male nor female."[36]

Every human being who came into existence should have been able to produce a city out of their being because of the Melchizedek principle within them. Jesus put it in the context of serving (the parable of the talents in Matthew 25:14-30). But where did the cities come from? The cities came from the sweat and life of the servant. So, when they gave their talent back, the master turned it into a city because it came out of their being.

It is interesting to note that Jesus even mentions that some people will have more cities than others. It is true that we will all receive the same reward and the same possessions. Jesus did give the parable of the workers in the field where the last were given the same reward as the first, but that has to do with salvation. Salvation is given equally, no matter when you enter.

This is very important for us to understand. We know that the origin of something indicates what the future must be. So, the Melchizedek idea also means that you and I will rule cities. Yet not just that — cities will be born out of us

---

36 Galatians 3:28

that are used as principles for the manifestation of creation in the future.

Let me quote a passage from scripture. It may not fit completely, but I want to quote it because the Holy Spirit just showed it to me in a flash. The passage says, "As a young man marries a bride, so shall your sons marry you [speaking to the land]."[37] This is a strange doctrine! We as sons are going to be married to a land! We are going to have a mutual interconnection with dominions, territories, and cities that will be married to us. These marriages will frame new creations. Let me emphasize again that we are born from above. All of us are born with a mother above who knows what our cities will bring forth. And I now believe that those cities given to us as the Melchizedek sons of God will have the capacity to bring forth things that are in the mind of God, which will astound us. It is God's intention for that city, through the light that we have become, to terraform and to shape a new world that constantly creates new worlds, and manifests glory upon glory upon glory.

When I was mildly complaining the other day, the King of kings reminded me and said, "You are a god." I said, "Yes." He said, "But I am the God of gods." Then He said, "You are a lord, my son," I said, "Yes, sir." "And I am the Lord of lords." You see, He had to remind me, "You are an authority." I said, "Yes." Then He said, "I am the Authority of authorities. I am still your Father." It was not like a genealogical account of my lineage — "I'm your father's brother's sister's uncle." No, He said, "I am your Father." So let us see how this works out for us. We are the reflection of the original intent of God. We can now return to that in order to carry out what was truncated — the restoration of creation as it relates to that which was created in conjunction with humanity at its

37   Isaiah 62:5

helm with God establishing humanity as the principle and the epitome of His creation.

Being Melchizedek priests grants us access to the complex possibilities of creation and enables God to reveal the mysteries of His being to us. This revelation is what I am discussing with you. Christ became one of us so that we could become like Him to God. Thus, as far as God is concerned, we are the Melchizedek Priesthood. However, now the Melchizedek Priesthood is not just a projection into creation; it is the Creator serving and leading our order. This means that God has become a part of our order, and we have become a part of God's Order, which is an eternal and uncreated order. I will not delve very far into the concept of "without mother, without father" right now, yet we must consider the genetic and transmutational potential within the Melchizedek principle. It includes what it means to rule in this world, not just a tribe, but on a cosmic scale. To have dominion over all the heavens and the earth, over principalities and powers, is all embodied in the Melchizedek principle.

All this is made possible by your having been born from above. When you were born from above, the Melchizedek genes were inserted into you. And when you are initiated by the infilling of the Holy Spirit, your Melchizedek consciousness, which is your God-consciousness, and your Melchizedek frequency, which is the God-frequency or the vibrational movement that we identify as the God-vibration, moves you in a higher way. It takes you more and more into the mind of God and the being of God. Melchizedek is the opening of the Divine to all of humanity, raising up human beings by cutting away tribal structures and all the things that keep humanity from becoming one with the Divine. However, when our arguments lead to division, where we seek to destroy each other and lie about each other, then we are not ready for the Melchizedek Priesthood. In the Melchizedek Priesthood, tribal loyalty, color loyalty, and racial loyalty begin to disappear.

It is amazing that we all talk about becoming one, yet we constantly, both in the oppressed and oppressor communities, maintain boundaries that prevent us from truly becoming Melchizedek priests. Only by removing the boundaries between Jew and Gentile, Jew and Greek, and male and female, and looking at our spiritual relationship as surpassing these physical things, can we achieve unity in Christ and become the "One New Man." The Melchizedek Priesthood will remain truncated unless we do this. The world has made national boundaries so strong that God probably allowed it so that we do not kill each other. But those who have come to experience this must begin to deal with those boundaries and draw humanity together.

The real threat of Christianity is its doctrine of brotherhood and being one family interconnected in spite of our natural differences. This unity is what is feared, not denominations or other doctrines. The threat is the manifestation of the seventh Adam who is the Adam of peace and rest in creation. This unity is the feared by the world because it means that they cannot control everything. This doctrine of unity proclaims to the world that there is a group of people who are looking beyond the so-called natural structures and are bringing Christ to manifestation, bringing God and man together, working towards the union and unity of humanity, bringing the future to the present, wiping out the bondage that the past has held on humanity, and releasing humanity into fullness of life.

However, like everything else, none of us should try to force all of humanity into this or claim that all human beings are there when they do not want to be. Some people do not want this unity. This is part of what we must understand — the Melchizedek Priesthood is not a warring, conquering, or destructive priesthood. Its only war is against the devil, the spirit of death, and the spirit of the fear of death that holds humanity in bondage. Once we overcome that, then those who believe will begin to manifest what they need to manifest. Amen!

Chapter 4
THE PRIESTHOOD OF ALL HUMANITY

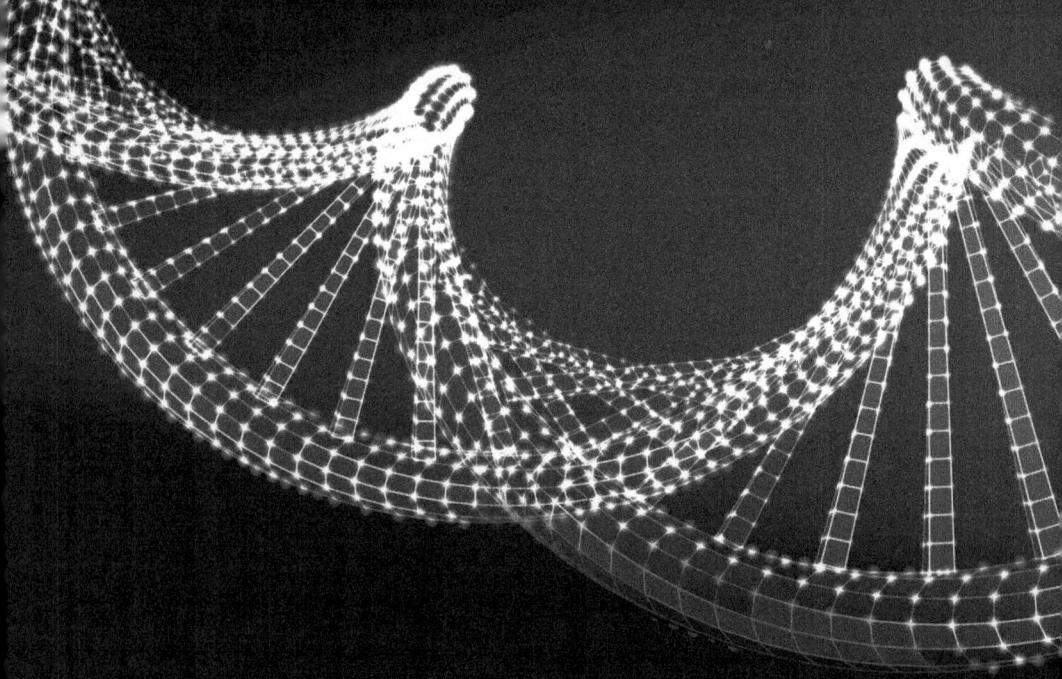

We have touched on a number of things, including the relationship between Jesus Christ, our Lord and Savior, and Melchizedek, which is powerfully described in scripture. We talked about the fact that Jesus Christ has been initiated into the order of Melchizedek by becoming a human being, which means that the order of Melchizedek is a human priesthood. It is not just a national or tribal priesthood; it is a priesthood given to all of humanity. The reason the Melchizedek Priesthood was given to Abraham was so that the Messiah, Jesus Christ, coming through the lineage of Abraham, would become the embodiment of the priesthood for all humanity. We speak of the priesthood of all believers, but this is actually the priesthood of all humanity.

The goal is for all of humanity to worship God through a human being, Jesus Christ, the Messiah. According to scripture, He became human and is the embodiment of all humanity. In the Messiah, all human beings participate in His humanity through His body and His divinity. All human beings have the capacity to participate in His divinity. The priesthood of all believers is the priesthood of all humanity, and this is called the Melchizedek principle.

This prototypical idea of humanity occurred in the mind of God before humans were physically created and is now being manifested in the person of Christ. He is all of humanity in one body, and He is also God in human form. In Him, there is the possibility of deification and having a divine body. In Him, humanity can become like God. In the body of Christ, we are given the opportunity to return to God's original idea about us as His inner thought.

To understand the Melchizedek Priesthood, one must look at the Messiah. It is one thing to have revelations about who Melchizedek is and have encounters with him in the realms of heaven, but it is important to remember that there are stories in various ancient literatures about Melchizedek and his manifestation in different beings in creation. These were temporary garments given for the purpose of embodying the idea of a priesthood for humanity, which is not the Levitical priesthood, although the Levitical priesthood still has a role to play and will be subsumed in the future through the Messiah.

A rabbi has written that the sons of David were priests, and those of us from a Hebrew background know that his sons were priests, but not of the Levitical order. Their priesthood was after the order of Melchizedek. I mentioned earlier that Solomon made sacrifices in the temple, but by what authority did he do so when other kings who tried to make sacrifices were punished by God? This illustrates to us that David had a specific connection to a priesthood that was not the Levitical priesthood. He structured the Levitical priesthood around the Melchizedek Priesthood. David and Solomon actually functioned as priests and served as examples of the kingly Melchizedek Priesthood.

So what can we learn from Solomon? In the case of David, we know his father, but we do not know his mother. In the case of Solomon, we know his father was David, but his mother is supposed to be a Gentile. So the priesthood that Solomon picked up is outside of the Levitical/Aaronic priesthood, even though he used traditional Israelite structures. Yet, when it came to major events, it was David and Solomon who made the sacrifices. In Israel, there had been no such combination of priest and king. The tribe that represented the priesthood was separate from the kingship, and there was a reason for that. Only a righteous person who knows God intimately can combine kingship and priesthood and care for the people. In Canaanite religion, they became tyrants and even sacrificed their own people. David was unique in that he never sacrificed any Israelites, no matter how difficult they were. He made that a principle of his kingship. Supposedly, a story is told about Melchizedek giving Abraham bread and wine. Some of the people that Abraham had just killed were the sons of the king of Salem. Remember that, as we have learned from the Lord Jesus Christ, wine represents renewal, forgiveness, and transmutation. It removes sin. There was a sense that the first Melchizedek knew exactly what Abraham had done in warfare. He gave Abraham communion and bread in order to purify and cleanse him so that he could continue the priesthood in his being and pass it on to his children. Remember what Jesus said when he took this cup, "This is the cup of the new covenant in my blood, which is shed for the remission of sins."[38] So, the wine is used in the context of atonement, forgiveness, and cleansing by the priest. Melchizedek was a priest, and the wine was a symbol of peacemaking and forgiveness.

Many rabbis believe that when Abraham took the bread and wine, Melchizedek transferred that which belonged to all of humanity over to Abraham, his seed, and his DNA to preserve it all the way to the Messiah. The Messiah does not come from a Levitical lineage; the Messiah comes from the tribe of Judah, and not from all of Judah. The Messiah does not come from the pure lineage of Israel. Those who argue against the involvement of Gentiles in the lineage of Israel will agree that at least four women in the lineage of Jesus were not Israelites, thereby reinserting the Melchizedek Priesthood not through the Levitical lineage but through the kingly lineage. This priesthood comes through different lineages that include people from different nations. We do not know how many other people are involved in the lineage of David like Ruth (a Moabite), Tamar, Bathsheba, and Rahab). The priesthood of all humanity was established through these bloodlines. When David spoke directly to his son Solomon saying, "verily thou art a priest after the order of Melchizedek,"[39] he was referring to what the kings of Israel transferred to their sons as they took over the kingship. This statement was given to every legitimate king of Israel from the tribe of Judah. So with the kingship came the statement of being a priest after the order of Melchizedek.

In Israel, there was a type of kingship that also carried a permanent priesthood, and then there was a priesthood that did not carry kingship, even though the priests may have dressed as kings. The garment was that of the king, but the

38   Matthew 26:28
39   Psalm 110:4

priesthood was temporary. It is only in the permanency of the kingship that the eternal priesthood is revealed, through the insertion of the DNA of Melchizedek who gave Abraham communion and inserted the principle into Abraham's DNA. This DNA transferred through all the kings of Israel to the Messiah, whom we call Yeshua. Incidentally, the Hebrews believe that the Messiah will be an actual Melchizedek priest.

I said earlier that every believer carries the Melchizedek DNA, which was activated at the new birth. However, it was inherent in the kingship of David, embodied in the fullness of the person of Christ, who is the son of God. I am not just speaking about a spiritual concept. I believe that an actual transfer took place when Melchizedek prayed for Abraham and gave him communion. Then, with the coming of the Messiah, the Melchizedek DNA came full circle and was returned to humanity through the person of Jesus Christ.

You and I have access to this Melchizedek Priesthood because God became human, and we are participating in it with Him. We are not only beholding His glory but participating in it as well. We have the Melchizedek gene. This means that we, who have come to Christ, have ceased to be temporarily conceived and have become eternally born. Some people argue that Melchizedek was a human being, but you cannot deny the fact that the Bible says he was without father or mother (not naturally born). Therefore, no Melchizedek priest is patterned according to the flesh; they have no beginning and no end.

The new birth is according to God. The Melchizedek Priesthood is the one that ministers to God directly by sharing in His nature. It is a divine participatory priesthood. The Melchizedek Priesthood serves God from God's own nature. In other words, they serve God as God. The purpose

of God becoming human was to minister to Himself through His own nature and perfection through humanity. As a Melchizedek priest, God makes you into His own self, so that your ministration to God will be, fundamentally, God's ministry to Himself.[40]

According to the book of Hebrews, the High Priest must constantly make sacrifices for his own sins. But what if the High Priest is completely perfect? This means that all the priests surrounding him are also made perfect. They do not minister from the perspective of guilt, blame, or condemnation, but from a position of divine embodiment. There is a complete saturation of Divinity in God ministering back to God's self. The gift is God gifting God's self, by God's self, back to God's self.

The Melchizedek Priesthood is a deified priesthood. If you have been divinized or deified by God and have become an embodiment of His being, then your ministration is God to God. The instrumentation of this priesthood is that God has become "all in all" in you, so your ministration is acceptable to God because He has made you a participant in His nature. Again, the Melchizedek Priesthood is a participatory priesthood and this participation is mutual.

Now let us address the aspect of Melchizedek as a carrier of this mystery of God. The Melchizedek priest, by ministering to God, also participate in ministering to human beings. We talked about the priesthood being mutual because you are now saturated, participating, and mutually entangled with God. Your priesthood ministers God to God. Yet God does not want to minister to God alone. Remember Ezekiel 40 describes three categories of priests: one that serves the house, one that serves the people, and one that serves God

40 Hebrews 7:27

directly. The one who serves God directly serves God and then takes his garment, places it in the presence of God, and turns around to minister to the people. In these priestly activities, we can see this mutual participation, and this is the real power of the Melchizedek Priesthood. God participates in you and ministers to God's self; it is not just one-sided. When God participates in you and saturates you, He also takes on your humanity, which means that God, by our mutual participation, ministers to humanity through you.

I think this is what is meant by the statement that even though the Most High sits in heaven, He still shows concern for the lowly. You and I are participating in a mutual ministry with God. God ministers to Himself as human (us) and then as Himself. He then ministers to Himself in us, through us, as Himself. Then he turns around and ministers to us as us while retaining His divinity.

So, in the Melchizedek Priesthood, we have the best of both worlds. When you read that the Melchizedek Priesthood was transferred to Abraham, you need to see why he did so and remember that it was not done by an Israelite, Hebrew, or Semite, but by a Canaanite. It is amazing that God is very clear that this belongs to all humanity. Melchizedek appeared not as a Semitic king or Hebrew king, but as a Canaanite king and priest — one who worshiped the Most High God, not idols. Abraham acknowledged that the God of Melchizedek and his God were the same. What a fascinating mystery!

I once decided to delve into the spiritual realm and ask questions about Melchizedek. As a Hebrew, I asked Melchizedek why he was present when Abraham encountered him and why he was among the Jebusites. I learned from him that he represents all of humanity and that his priesthood is for all human beings. If he had not appeared at that time

as a Gentile, then some group of people would have been excluded from the coming of the Messiah. Melchizedek informed me that he had appeared in almost all tribes, trying to steer them away from idolatry. Whenever you find a priest in history who renounced idolatry, you find a human-divine movement towards the arrival of the Messiah. Being without father or mother and having access to the eternal essence of God means that God does not want to do anything without you. God does not want to rule the world without you, not because He cannot, but because He chooses not to create more worlds without your participation. Again, we see that the Melchizedek Priesthood is a participatory priesthood through which the priest embodies the Divine and manifests the divine intent in creation.

I asked the Father, "Why do You want to allow Yourself to struggle through humanity when You could do it on Your own?" God could have created the world on His own, even though we were present, but He chose to bring us into the process and participate. I asked why He chose to do it this way, and the Father answered that it was because He wanted to. He could have just commanded, but then we would never become like Him, just being a tool in His hand. If He made us like Him and never allowed us to experience the process of becoming like Him, we would end up like the other guy. So this is why we have the mutuality embedded in the Melchizedek Priesthood. He could have saved us from His throne in heaven, but God chose a dimensional process because of His love for us.

Now, let us move on to the superiority of the Melchizedek system over angels. It is important to note that angels cannot serve as priests to God. Angels worship, they are doors, and they magnify God, but they are not priests to God. Only human beings can be priests according to scripture. An angel would have to become a human being in order to be a priest. This was part of the problem with the Noah generation. They wanted to become human so that they could be the embodiment and carrier of all that the Melchizedek Priesthood carries. They saw the human priesthood through Melchizedek as being superior because it is a direct ministration of God back to God's self through humanity, as we see in Jesus Christ our Lord. Therefore, Christ, being part of the Melchizedek Priesthood, is superior to angels. Angels serve in purity, yet God chose humanity and this system to manifest the full measure of His service.

The Melchizedek system is not a copy. We forget that the Melchizedek Priesthood is an actual priesthood. It was the original intent of God to participate in the release of the life of the Lamb that caused the universe to exist. So, it is not a copy, and neither are you. You are the reality of the original.[41] There is no such thing as a copy when it comes to what God does; everything is an original. The Melchizedek Priesthood is not a type in the sense that we use the term "type." It is actually the reality of the priesthood. If it were a copy, then Jesus Christ would not be able to become a member of it. The reason Jesus Christ is part of the Melchizedek Priesthood is because it is the real, original priesthood. Everyone who is a Melchizedek priest is the full manifestation of all the powers of the original, invested in that being.

Being a part of the participatory priesthood means participating with God in creation as well as participating in directing how angels function within creation in relation to humanity. Did you know that it was through David and the Melchizedek Priesthood that the knowledge of how to

41   You can find this teaching and many others at www.aactev8.com

open the 24 gates of the earth was set in motion? The whole purpose of the Tabernacle that David built was to open up the 24 dimensions of earthly creation and align them with the 24 gateways, which parallel the original city that came out of the side of the Lamb. The power of the Melchizedek Priesthood aligns the earth, symbolizing humanity, with the 24 gateways, which correspond to the 24 hours of the original city.

The earth desires the Melchizedek priest to stand in their rightful place. Once our consciousness rises, the earth will align itself with the 24 gateways and dimensions of the original city, freeing the earth to fulfill its destiny. The glory of the Lord is not a fleeting or misty presence, but rather human beings will cover the earth like water covers the sea. When human beings manifest the glory and its vibrational frequency which is connected to the Melchizedek Priesthood and when it fills the earth, the earth's consciousness will rise to its intended level. In an instant, everything that has been lost from the earth will be restored, including trees and other necessary reflections of the original city. By aligning ourselves with the Melchizedek Priesthood through Jesus Christ, we ensure that every new earth that arises will immediately receive the results of what has happened on earth without undergoing the same process. This is also what is meant by the phrase "For the earnest expectation of the creation waiteth for the revealing of the sons of God."[42] Every priest is a mediator, and we mediate into creation the Divine that has become us. The earth and all of creation receives that vibrational frequency, and every new earth will align itself and receive what has already been manifested.

Let us take a step back into creation. When God created the earth, He said it was very good, and when He created

42 Romans 8:19

humanity, the earth continued to be developed. The book of Ephesians says that until we all come to maturity in Christ, we are the final Adam continuing the work of God on earth.

If our priesthood reaches maturity and we become the final Adam, then all the earth-like planetary systems in all the galaxies in the universe will hear our frequency and immediately manifest what God originally intended for the earth. It is up to us, and God will use us to do so. God wants to use us to carry out His plans, and He wants to participate in us as we participate in Him. It is important to understand the fullness of the Melchizedek Priesthood because being a Melchizedek priest means more than just saying it. With this priesthood, we no longer need to seek ways to get into the presence of God because through Christ, who became all of humanity, we have a door and direct access to Divinity.

It is mind-boggling to think that this priesthood is not mentioned much in scripture, yet it is actually mentioned more than many topics that we have turned into doctrines. For example, this priesthood is mentioned in Genesis, the Psalms, and in passing in the book of Ezekiel. Although Zadok became the Sadducees, Zadok was actually a Melchizedek priest. God said that the sons of Zadok who did not follow their idols would minister to Him and come to Him.[43] So the Zadok principle was meant to operate in the Melchizedek Priesthood. It is noteworthy that even in the New Testament, the Sadducees, who have received a bad reputation, were descendants of Zadok. They had turned everything into legality and rejected the supernatural. This presents a problem when discussing the Sadducees. The sons of Zadok should have carried out the Melchizedek Priesthood within Israel since they were descendants of Zadok who was put in charge by David.

43 Ezekiel 44:15

Throughout the history of Israel, there was a constant tension between two groups vying for the High Priestly role — one descended from Eli and the other from Zadok. The kings also knew that they were priests after the order of Melchizedek. Although the Zadokites were not the direct lineage of the people who should have been the priests, this issue is a complex and academic topic that can be set aside for now.

When we consider the significance of the Melchizedek Priesthood, we must understand that, when a Melchizedek priest arises, they have the ability to activate the gates of the ancient city, allowing for the terraforming of exoplanets and other planetary systems. As this consciousness arises, all the galaxies with their planetary systems will come into the reality of their intended manifestation. This includes a restoration of the genuine relational principles that are based on human DNA and human rulership of creation through which all order must be subordinate to human beings through the rulership of the one true High Priest after the order of Melchizedek. We are discussing an interconnected trans-dimensionality that is inherent in the participatory nature of the Melchizedek Priesthood. Again, as you know, through it humanity participates with Divinity and God participates in man.

If this is the case, it means that the Melchizedek Priesthood is a cosmic priesthood. By cosmic, I mean more than just the cosmos. I mean it is cosmic in the sense that its fragrance and its movement are in every cosmos. All of stars and galaxies in the cosmos know this priesthood because it participated in their foundational emergence even before it became a reality.

If you take the DNA of a believer and place it in an empty space, the star system that forms in that region will vibrate according to the Melchizedek DNA within the believer. The Order of Melchizedek is a powerful thing and it is important for believers to get involved physically and put their genetic imprint on everything that leaves Earth and goes into space. This is because there is something in our DNA that we can use to move spiritually, but we also need to participate physically. This is where the importance of physical participation lies. We can create many things through physical and spiritual participation. This may surprise you, but a physical being with DNA can still walk into a spiritual atmosphere and mess it up. It is mysterious. The reason God became human is because it was necessary to place physical DNA within the context of spirit. God made the DNA for God's sake even though it is fallen now. He made it as a record-keeping, record-transferring information system to form and frame worlds.

Within that DNA are hidden structures of world formation, world framing, and world manifestations. DNA is incredible stuff. In other words, it has a cosmic nature. Because of where it is now in Christ, this DNA carries the Melchizedek genes and this overcoming victory-oriented power. This is what is meant when the scripture says, "The light shines in darkness, and the darkness cannot overcome it."[44] No chaos is possible due to the framing power within the Melchizedek order.

If you subject any molecular structure in any realm to the light power of the Melchizedek Priesthood, it will orient itself towards the light. This means that the light shines in darkness and the darkness cannot overcome it. Ultimately then, the Melchizedek Priesthood carries this overcoming, victorious power, which is based on who the High Priest of this order is. If Jesus Christ is the Lord and the High Priest

44 John 1:5

after the order of Melchizedek, it means that everything said about Him becomes part of the lives of everyone who participates in that order. His genetic structure has the capacity to overcome every darkness and reorient every chaos towards divine order. This is how John states it: "Whoever has been born of God overcomes the world."[45]

I once had a dream about a guy who entered into space and went to a world where the beings there had created chaos because of their hatred for God's spiritual realm. However, this guy carried within himself a sound that, when released, reoriented the entire area according to the Melchizedek frequency. As a result, a sweet fragrance filled the arena, causing all the chaos-creating beings to shift away from the center of the exploding light and movement in that region of space. I witnessed as this movement transformed darkness into light. Despite this, some beings still chose to belong to the darkness and moved away, but the entire region was completely transformed.

So it is an overcoming victory because of the High Priest. In the natural realm in which we find ourselves, it overcomes entropy, meaning it does not decay, and it overcomes anything that causes decay. This means that when Christ became one of us and joined our order, He inserted himself into us to overcome the decaying power of sin. This power is based not only on ordinary acts of sin but also on unbelief and idolatry. Instead of worshiping something we have made into an idol, we worship the God who has become us, and He directs his worship through us back to Himself.

When a human being turns away from the source of light, the God of light, to something else, it removes the principle of light. But when the principle of light, the Melchizedek genetic principle, is activated and shines, it caused Noah and his brother to shine like the light.

Noah was the first one to be called a priest. According to the second apocryphal book of Enoch,[46] a child was born in the time of Noah to a barren, dying old woman named Sopanim. In fact, she was the wife of Nir, Noah's brother, and they did not know how she conceived. Nir was ashamed of her and tried to send her away because he did not believe her story. However, Sopanim cried out to Nir that the day of her death had arrived and she died right in front of him. Nir and Noah wrapped her in a shroud and planned to bury her in secret. While they were off digging the grave, the child was born and it was a full-grown child, around three years old! Noah realized that the child had the badge of priesthood on his chest and that his birth was a sign that the Lord was restoring the priesthood in their bloodline. They named the child Melchizedek. According to the story, when the child was born, God told Noah that the flood was coming and sent Michael (or Gabriel, depending on the account) to take him to paradise and keep him there until the flood was over.

Now some have argued that Melchizedek was actually Shem, Noah's son. However, I do not agree that Melchizedek was Shem because, according to Enoch, Melchizedek was Nir's son, not Noah's. This does not mean Shem did not learn from Melchizedek since Melchizedek existed before Shem was born and lived in paradise before coming back to Earth. He was not naturally conceived. If you want to use typology, he is a type of Christ that was not conceived through human possibility but through divine possibility, taking the original human DNA and putting it into the womb of Mary. However, you could also argue that, as Melchizedek in the mind of God was the key to the creation of the world, he was also the key

46 2 Enoch 71

to the creation of Adam and the seeding of Mary's being. Otherwise, how could Mary's son be Melchizedek unless he comes from the original archetypal Adam? That is who Melchizedek is — the Adam before Adam.

The ideal Adam in the mind of God was actually a reality that could be projected as the priest who oversaw the release of life from the Lamb to create the world. This same priest must come at the end of days to restore all humanity who believe in their priesthood, enabling the creation of new worlds and beyond. God intended for Melchizedek to come and for us to become an embodiment of the Melchizedek Priesthood. That is why He made Himself our High Priest. Hallelujah, glory be to God!

So we need to enter the Melchizedek Age. The Order of Melchizedek is the order originally taught by God into which all humanity enters. It is an overcoming, victorious priesthood; it is a light-infusing priesthood, a decay-removing priesthood, and it releases divine technology into creation, drawing from its hidden divine secrets. Melchizedek blessed Abraham, saying, "Blessed be Abraham by the Most High God." Only the Melchizedek Priesthood can invoke such blessings upon creation, releasing the entrapped essence and light of God, revealing Divinity throughout all of creation.

Chapter 5

MELCHIZEDEK TECHNOLOGIES

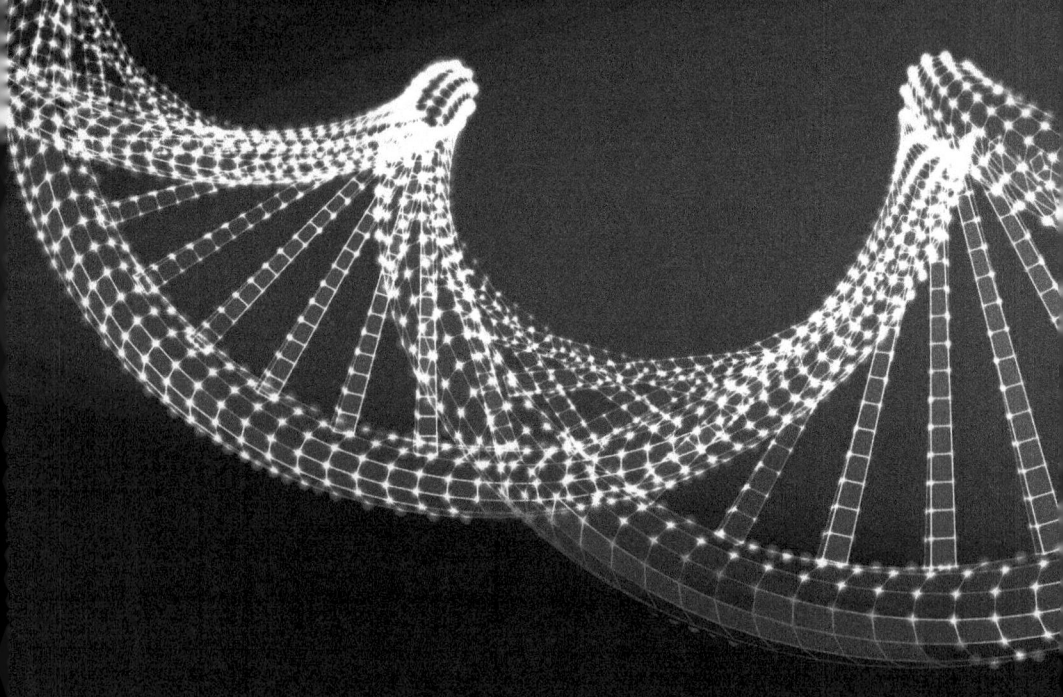

So the Lamb of God, which was laid down before the foundation of the world, was slain. We have established that it was not the Father who slew the Lamb, nor was it the Father who slew the Son when He came into the world. It was humanity, and you can deduce that from the projected principle of humanity. The Lamb could not have slain itself, as that would be suicide and the sacrifice would be meaningless.

The giving has to come willingly, but it must be implemented by someone other than the Father and other than the victim itself. A goat does not slay itself on the altar, nor does a sheep. A priest does so, and to do that, you require a priest. God did not allow Abraham to officiate as a priest in the slaying of his son.

Based on all my vision experiences with Melchizedek who encompasses all of humanity in their pre-manifestation state, I was able to deduce that the participated in releasing the life of the Lamb before the foundation of the world to create the corona of blood that holds creation from collapsing back into the mind of God. In this state, creation can be experienced, touched, and remain in the created space. The Lamb of God is the one who actually performs this task, and this pattern repeats itself throughout creation.

In the new creation, the Holy Spirit works with us in the same manner. The blood of Jesus Christ first saturates our hearts, which is a metaphor for our being. Then when the Holy Spirit enters into our being and becomes a part of who we are, it does not completely obliterate us because the blood acts as our protection until we merge with the movement of the Holy Spirit and our entire being is intertwined. The blood not only protects us from sin but also keeps us from being completely erased by the power of God. God does not want to completely eliminate the form He gave us originally. Instead, He wants to fill us and have a reflexive relationship with us. So part of what happened in the Melchizedek Priesthood was the release of the blood, but the blood was released as light, as I have discussed in other teachings.

Coming back to the principle of Melchizedek, we talked a bit about how the non-decaying principle functions for us. I do not want to call it the Melchizedek consciousness because for us to function at that level, it has to be a God consciousness, a level of divine consciousness, a God thought, or a God process. This is because the Melchizedek Priesthood, in a sense, is a channel for manifesting God's thoughts, God's principles, God's consciousness, and God's movement in creation.

Learning from David, we can see how he structured things according to the Melchizedek principle and we understand that the city can adjust itself according to the pattern of the day of that realm in which we serve. The reason the city displays the Earth in 24 dimensions is because man on Earth operates in a six-day principle. If man were to move and live on Mars, the city would arrange itself towards a 36 gateway dimensional principle, which is the trading floor of nine (3+6=9). The earth affects everything in creation, but some things in creation must receive their point of movement at the nine points. I will not delve into that right now, but we must understand that the earth will affect everything in creation.

Now, let us come back to dealing with this in creation. If the social and political arena we are in right now does not reveal righteousness and is not structured according to divine justice, it is because the believers are not expressing the Melchizedek Priesthood. The Melchizedek Priesthood is not just about shouting and screaming in the spiritual realm. The Melchizedek Priesthood for us in this realm must be incarnational; it must be embodied. David and Solomon, Melchizedek Priesthood along with what we have seen in Israel, are the epitome of the manifested Melchizedek Priesthood. Every true king manifests it.

Let us look from the beginning: Adam, as a Melchizedek priest, had a formative or form-giving technology. Adam

gave form to all the animals we see today. Some of them have been given form by the thought of humanity within creation, and some have disappeared due to human activity. When humanity returns to the Order of Melchizedek, many of the endangered and extinct species that are good for humanity will begin to reappear, and technologies for the restoration of creation (*Tikkun Olam*) will emerge. True Melchizedek kingship can actually change the environmental ecology by the way it vibrates across creation, but it will also receive technology for doing so.

When we shift to the same technology that Adam used, which is a breath technology that is Melchizedek-oriented and word-activated, it is connected to the various bodies that humanity is able to activate. A glorified body, for example, has a way of using words that allow for the manifestation of higher realities, and a saved body has an embedded capacity for using words to manifest certain things. A natural body has the ability to use words or ideas to bring about certain outcomes. The Melchizedek body, by virtue of its priesthood, is able to release the life of the word, creating an environment for the manifestation of God's own word, bringing to life what God intended. This means that the more we embody the Melchizedek Priesthood, the more we move in the Melchizedek realm, and the more we develop the technology of Adam, which is the technology of giving form to created things.

Remember, there is a difference between what was created and what was manifested, as we find in Genesis 2. The world was created, but it was not yet fully manifested. Things existed, but they were not on Earth until man arrived. It is through worship, which is through word, that the Melchizedek Priesthood has a specific kind of technology that allows for the manifestation or formation of what is in the realm of ideas. So, we see Adam doing that, and we see Adam using names and word technology.

I am drawn to the Greek word *onomazó*,[47] which refers to giving things a name and defining them through words. This is what we are already doing with computers. We are using them to create codes or rather words that shape and form things. We have come a long way from the days of simple emojis, and now we have complex systems. That is why I recommend that believers learn to code and delve into scientific pursuits. They should not only learn how to code genes but also how to code environments. It is important for us to understand how to use both spoken and abstract language and thought systems to create environments that support righteous technologies and actions. This is the future, and the question is whether believers will be a part of it or simply follow the world and create the same things.

The technology of the future is going to be advanced due to the increased understanding and resurgence of the principles of the Melchizedek Priesthood. As more people come to know Yeshua and leave idolatry, the technology of Melchizedek is emerging. In comparison to what we have experienced in the past 100 years, the advancements that will come through the Melchizedek principle will seem like living in a different world. However, to fully utilize and understand these advancements, the righteous genetic structure of the Melchizedek Priesthood, which is the word and life of the Messiah, must be integrated through those who believe in Him and embody His teachings, not just imitate them.

Just like God put Adam in charge of tending the garden and tilling the ground, he was still instructed to till the

---

47 https://biblehub.com/greek/3687.htm. Onomazó ὀνομάζω I give a name to, mention, call upon the name of.

ground even after he was removed from the garden. The cultivation of the earth involves the technological ability to extract what is inherent in nature. The earth is not just the physical soil; it encompasses everything. Very few believers have already begun to cultivate the earth in this sense or to operate in this way.

If the goal is for humanity to become like Adam and for believers to become the ultimate Adam, then the Melchizedek principle must start to manifest the technology of Adam. This includes the capacity for self-regeneration, the ability to put the body in a state of sleep and awaken it, to put the body in stasis and re-insert the soul, and to re-enter the body. The concept of putting the body in stasis through spiritual and meditative processes, which we have been teaching for years, is now being explored in movies,. One day, we will discuss the technologies of the Melchizedek era. One of the major technologies of this era is putting the body in stasis, and I believe this is why meditation has become so popular around the world. We must be able to bring the body to a state where it can be in stasis and allow the person to do what they need to do next in the future.

The body will eventually go, but for now it is important to renew its energetic structures. This was part of Adam's technology. Before he fell, he had the ability to lay down and take his life back up again. In our case, we experience perpetual resurrection through the death of one person, allowing for continuous renewal of our physical bodies. This is what the Bible refers to when it says, "One who dies at a hundred years shall be considered a youth."[48]

This mechanistic principle indicates that we have the capacity to overcome decay when it is operating properly.

48 Isaiah 65:20

Many believers could have died when they were 35 years old. However, because they are believers, the Melchizedek gene is activated in them and has kept them alive until the age of 70 or 80. This phenomenon deserves closer examination. The record of people who are still alive despite their age shows the power of the Melchizedek principle. This principle serves as a renewing force, as it is the life of Christ within the individual. It demonstrates the perpetual priesthood of Christ that has become the Melchizedek garment we put on ourselves. This allows us to thrive and have longevity, thanks be to God Who gives us continuous victory through Jesus Christ our Lord!

I want to mention an Adamic technology called the technology of Seth, which is a technology of rest. This is rest in the name of YHVH, as it was when Seth was born that men began to call upon the name of Yahweh. This is a continuation of the technology of Adam, using the Name and frequency of the Name to bring things to pass. The scripture repeatedly mentions "in my name," indicating the power of the name of Yahweh to control elements and structure them for miracles. These miracles include healing the sick, raising the dead, and other signs and wonders. In the future, there will be technological miracles created by people who can simply speak a word.

There will come a time when technology allows for healing through the use of the name of Yahweh. By speaking the Name and embedding it into a technology, individuals can enter into a chamber and receive healing, even if they do not have the power to speak the word or if there is not someone present to speak for them. The Ark of the Covenant was a technology that could be entered into, allowing the body of the High Priest to be renewed by traveling to another dimension and returning to this one. However, it required a garment and a technology. The priestly garment renewed the body, while the transfer to other dimensions renewed life. The High Priest experienced the Melchizedek principle within a priesthood that was not of the Melchizedek Order. As we move into the consciousness of Melchizedek, it is expected that these types of healing technologies will be created by infusing chambers with the names and structures of God. This is where the Melchizedek Priesthood with its embodiment of the Divine and knowledge of the names of God comes into play.

The technology on the horizon will use the names of God, with Yahweh as the foundation, as a means to create miracles, signs, and wonders. As I mentioned before, this technology can be used to create healing chambers, and even medicine, infused with the power of God's name. When humanity fully embraces the Melchizedek Priesthood, the presence of God's name will keep decay at bay and bring about the continuous renewal of the human body. This technology was revealed in creation, and people began to call upon the name of the Lord. The birth of Seth marked a turning point in which technologies were created, but unfortunately, some of these technologies were misused. However, through the Melchizedek Priesthood, these technologies are used for the praise and glory of God and for the benefit of humanity, not for its destruction.

If the temple is ever rebuilt on earth, it will serve as a chamber for the continuous renewal of the human body, where those who worship there will renew their strength. The Melchizedek Priesthood will ensure that these technologies are used properly, bringing about a new era of miracles and wonders for the glory of God.

Chapter 6

BIBLICAL EXAMPLES

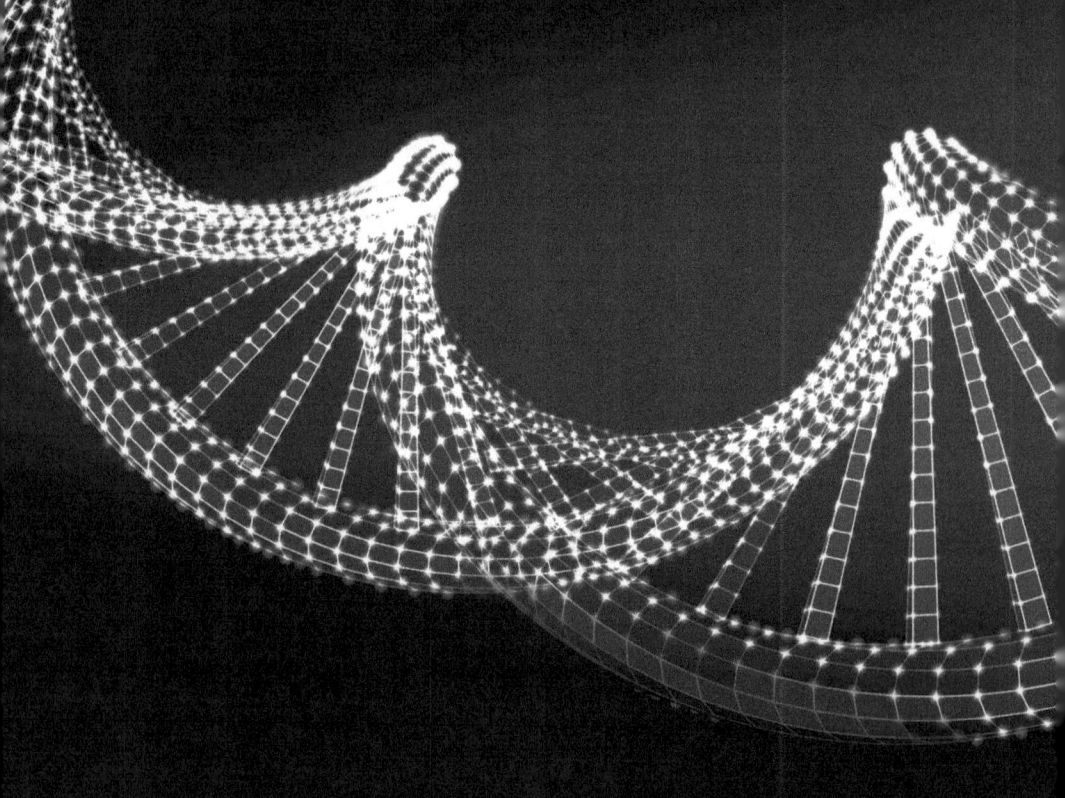

We will now discuss several Biblical examples of
Melchizedek priests. If you look at all the Melchizedek
priests, there was a movement of wealth that happened.
To summarize, God turned over all of creation and the
responsibility of its survival to Adam because he was the
Melchizedek "heir apparent."

The Melchizedek priest has the capacity to tap into the realm of divine provision and its fullness. This is revealed in scripture in many ways because the Melchizedek Priesthood operates by manifesting from the seat of rest. In fact, if you look at all the Melchizedek priests in scripture, you will see that they brought this movement and manifestation of wealth along with them.

Enoch represents transportation and transmutational technologies. We are moving beyond the traditional methods of structuring elements and are now doing so through our relationship with God. This led to the development of advanced technologies such as bilocation, translocation, and movement at the speed of light. The Melchizedek Priesthood is embedded with this principle of light. Therefore, it is important for believers to be involved in all aspects of society and not separate themselves so that they can infuse the life of God into burgeoning technologies. This comes from having a relationship with God. It means that we are now moving into the realm of transport and what some may consider science fiction. However, it is important to remember that things are only considered impossible because they have not yet been tried or achieved. The technology is moving at the speed of thought, and this is how Enoch was able to travel to other galaxies. His book mentions that he used a machine, but it was the combination of his thoughts with the technology that allowed him to travel at that speed. This highlights the importance of having pure thoughts that are connected to God's thoughts in order to infuse technology properly.

So if we travel at the speed of thought, it means that when we think of something, we are already there. Technology is coming that will be connected to the thought of man and it will occur so fast that the highest technology we can achieve today will look like child's play.

For example, someone can disappear while you are talking to them and they can show up instantly in India. This demonstrates the power of thought processes hidden in the Melchizedek Priesthood. What was once hidden within the Hebraic Priesthood is now being returned to humanity through belief in Christ, who will release it to the earth in this moment.

Noah Melchizedek Priesthood was also able to construct technologies by operating in the Melchizedek Priesthood. When there was a disaster on earth, God chose a man who was a priest in the order of Melchizedek, and whose family were also priests in the order of Melchizedek, to build the ark. To build the ark, Noah needed to have knowledge of mathematics, carpentry, and some level of chemistry and physics. God told him what it was going to look like and what he was supposed to do. Then Noah measured it and built it using dimensional numbers, which allowed it to transport from this realm to another realm.

The ark built by a Melchizedek priest was the first interdimensional craft that moved through the flood and into another place, a small space that became expansive and opened doors to all the dimensions. It is believed that Noah was a Melchizedek priest since there was no Jewish priesthood at the time. The Melchizedek Priesthood is an artisanal and fabricative priesthood with a focus on technology and knowledge, as illustrated by the story of Noah. The ark was not just a physical structure, but also an interdimensional craft that transported from one realm to another using dimensional numbers. This highlights the fact that the Melchizedek Priesthood is a technological priesthood, with the ability to formulate and build technologies to solve human problems and ensure humanity's survival during catastrophes.

If the Melchizedek Priesthood does not arise, technology may be created that does not promote human survival and can even lead to the loss of humanity. However, with the Melchizedek Priesthood, human beings can thrive and survive with the help of technologies revealed by God. Throughout history, the Melchizedek Priesthood has been essential in giving humanity a fresh start at every epoch and age.

So the Melchizedek Priesthood is a vocational priesthood, not just limited to full-time ministry. It is important to put this into a vocational context. Jesus was referred to as a carpenter, and Paul was referred to as a tent maker. You see, being a Melchizedek priest means incorporating your calling into your daily work, whether you are a scholar, psychologist, student, or something else. The High Priest in Israel also had to study different languages, understand different systems, and be knowledgeable about the science of sacrifices. He had to understand the appearance of blood, the timing of sacrifices, and the consequences if the systems were not aligned. This was his vocation, and he spent most of his life studying and reading the Torah to gain a deeper understanding. Most people must be taught this knowledge, rather than relying solely on inspiration.

The Bible mentions that Abraham "made souls and wealth."[49] I often wonder about the technology that Abraham used to make souls and all the animals he had. Although I am not sure yet, I believe that before he became a Melchizedek priest, Abraham developed successful methods of warfare and stood against the unrighteous by overcoming and defeating kings and protecting the poor.

We need believers in the military as righteous warriors, in the police force as righteous influences, and in the political

49 Genesis 12:5

process so that their spirits can infuse these areas according to the pattern promised by God. We need to make sure that we understand how these technologies work and so we will continue discussing Abraham and all that he accomplished.

Isaac's technology was manifested in farming. As mentioned in the Bible, Isaac planted and he harvested a hundredfold.[50] It is important to remember these things from scripture. Isaac was part of the Melchizedek Priesthood, although the Levitical priesthood had not been established yet and was transferred to his father. So, if Melchizedek priests are farmers, they have the ability to work with the seeds of the earth and their original, powerful, healing properties. Unfortunately, many believers have left farming and complain about the chemicals in food, but they are not growing food themselves. What if believers returned to growing food and restored the seeds to their natural state, bringing back their capacity for healing and helping the human body to be made whole? The seeds in creation would then respond to the Melchizedek vibration and once again bring restoration to humanity through our food.

It may sound simple, but the Melchizedek Priesthood is a holistic priesthood that takes into account technologies for transforming agriculture. We cannot stop complaining about the food we eat if we are not encouraging other believers to become farmers as well. Not everyone will become a farmer, but we cannot ignore the impact of this area of technology on our health and well-being. Yes, we can pray over food, but what if we do not have to pray for the food to be purified and cleansed? We just give thanks for it because the people who grow it have put life in it. We cannot talk about a priesthood that is creation-oriented while ignoring the things that actually help us and creation to function effectively. Our

50 Genesis 26:12

vibrational frequency is supposed to affect creation, but so far, the people who are affecting creation are the ones who actually want to mess up the human genetic structure and manipulate what happens to us. We are praying, but if we do not have someone stationed in a farm setting where seeds receive the vibrational frequencies of our prayers, we are missing something in the process. Remember, God put Adam in the garden so that Adam's vibrational frequency would continue to help the plants that God had created and continue the movement toward their original intent.

Do you have the account of Jacob breeding the speckled, spotted, and black sheep that would serve as his wages from Laban? Jacob's technology for genetic mutation and transformation was crude, but he was able to create healthy genes. According to the story, he did it through Yahweh. While some may view his methods as rudimentary or superstitious, it is important to note that he was successful in creating healthy genes. As a priest after the order of Melchizedek, he was able to use his knowledge and relationship with God to create positive change.

While some may criticize genetic splicing to remove disease, it is crucial that believers become involved in the field and engage with it from a righteous perspective. Without believers participating, the field will continue to advance without regard for preserving humanity. The ultimate goal is for humanity to live in the context of divinity and for the body to be transmuted into light. Until that time, genetic diseases can be removed through technological processes. The Melchizedek Priesthood plays a critical role in directing these processes towards God's original intent for humanity. Believers who are knowledgeable in genetics, biogenetics, biochemistry, and biotechnology are needed to effectively direct these fields towards that end.

The technology is going to come and those who study and understand it will have control over how the world works. If more of us were involved in fields like epidemiology and virology, we would not be passively observing what others are doing, but we would be actively figuring out ways to counter any perceived problems in the process. The principles of the Melchizedek Priesthood can become actual technologies in creation, with spiritual concepts becoming physical manifestations. We can see this in the incarnation of different aspects of creation. This includes the physical manifestation of the technologies used by the sons of Jacob when they were in Egypt, such as splitting mountains in two with their voice, redirecting rivers to water areas in need, and commanding the planting of trees to transform deserts. This was possible before the rise of the Levitical tribe, as the Aaronic priesthood did not yet exist.

Let us move now into the principle of kingship. Moses functioned as a Melchizedek priest until Aaron was set up. The Aaronic Priesthood was taken over by the sons of Aaron and was maintained by them. Until then, Moses served as both a king and a priest, as stated in the Bible. He was a king and a judge in Jeshurun, another name for Israel.[51] Moses' life began with a technological creation by his mother, who put him in a boat, or ark, in the Nile River. It is interesting to consider why no one saw the baby until Pharaoh's daughter found him. It is possible that there was a cloaking technology involved, as suggested by the Star Trek TV series. Cloaking technology would explain how the ark could have been in the Nile for a while without being noticed by anyone other than Pharaoh's daughter.

Placed directly by the mother, Moses began his life in the context of a creation technology. He performed signs and

51 Deuteronomy 33

wonders in the spiritual realm, curing physical diseases by the word of his mouth or the wave of his hand. The physical problems were created and removed by God through Moses' body and hand. Although Moses spoke to God, there were times when God told him to raise his staff and the problem would go away or come. This indicates that the staff must have carried a vibrational frequency that could change the environment for better or worse.

It is important that we discuss these things. I know some of you might think, "Oh, let's talk about mysteries," but this is a mystery. If these technologies do not affect life, and if your children cannot walk into an office and manifest divine patterns and produce technology, and if they cannot direct the words of technology in the way it should go, then the world will still be the same, and you will still struggle against the world. Many of the struggles we have are because of our inability to use these technologies.

Let us talk about the builders of the Ark of the Covenant for a moment. Do you know the name Bezalel? God showed Moses the technology in heaven and sent him to Bezalel who could build it.[52] Moses was a Levite, but Bezalel was from the tribe of Judah. Do you notice what is happening here? The technology for building the Ark of the Covenant came from the people who carried the Melchizedek Priesthood and would carry the line of Israelite kings. So the Ark was actually built by the tribe of kingship.

King David, a Melchizedek priest, devised fourteen different inventions to enhance worship through tuned frequencies. In fact, David made many inventions because of his knowledge of Melchizedek technology. God bless David van Koevering, one of the contemporary believers I knew

52 Exodus 35

who built a keyboard and tuned it to a specific vibrational frequency.[53] We need to encourage young people to develop such technologies that can enhance worship and spirituality. David made many contributions in this area.

Did you know that Solomon studied everything? Solomon was a polyglot and studied all kinds of things. According to the book of Proverbs, he wrote about botany, insects, animals, creatures, stars, the moon, and different dimensions. He wrote about medicine and pharmacy, including how to make perfumes and other things. It is said that much of what Solomon wrote is now lost, and if he were in this world today, we would call him a genius. He was brilliant and a priest, offering thousands of oxen before the Lord. He had access to this brilliant knowledge, some of which is no longer available. He studied ants, hornets, eagles, birds, and creeping things. He even delved into philosophy and observed human behavior. But not only that, Solomon developed technologies for manifestation.

You have already heard about making gold through alchemy, as it is said that Solomon carried the Melchizedek gene and is a priest forever after Melchizedek. It is important for us to understand that we can take up our vocational priesthood and manifest our Melchizedek nature, not just through preaching from the pulpit, but also by studying various subjects, including philosophy. I recently saw a news story about a child who graduated with a doctorate in philosophy from Cambridge or Oxford at the age of seven or eight. However, most believers do not encourage their children to pursue such academic paths. Instead, if the child shows an aptitude for preaching, they are often encouraged to pursue that instead. It is important for believers to recognize the potential of their children and steer them towards

53   www.heavensphysics.com/davidvankoevering/

careers where they can effectively contribute to society and transmute ideas into reality.

Samuel was a child when God called him and he lived in the temple. The temple was a training ground for various things such as how to structure sacrifice, how to run society, and more. It was not just limited to temple ministry. Samuel ended up running the nation and played a crucial role in forming the kingship of David. Despite not being a descendant of Eli or a priest, Samuel was able to access the Melchizedek principle and become a prophet, priest, and even a king in Israel. He also helped David develop technologies that assisted David in becoming the king. This is why David mourned Samuel when he died because Samuel was not only a prophet but also played a crucial role in David's reign. David mourned Samuel because Samuel was David's mentor and he mentored him on how to be a priest and a king.

It is remarkable that David's mentor was not a High Priest from the house of Levi, but someone from outside who served from a Melchizedek dimension. This is important to understand because the Melchizedek Priesthood is not just a temple-based priesthood. As I have said before, it is a cosmic, socio-political, technological, socio-chemical, biochemical, scientific, inventive, developmental, productive, engineering, and medical priesthood. It encompasses a wide range of fields and various aspects of society and is true physician priesthood. This priesthood is not limited to a certain location but is both localized and cosmic in nature. It has the ability to transform and transmute society to the glory and praise of God and is an amazing aspect of the divine plan for humanity.

I do not mean to bore you, but it is important that you understand how this works. It should come as no surprise that Jesus was born in the house of a carpenter and Joseph, his earthly father, was a Kabbalistic alchemist who used numbers and construction to manifest the glory of God. God placed his son with a builder. I know this may be difficult to understand because people often think that the only way to serve God is by singing in church or leading worship among believers. But this continuous belittling of people who serve as teachers, who transform the world, and bring the essence of God to others must stop. The priesthood of Melchizedek is about participating in creation.

Our presence is important, but it is not just important in the church. It is important in the transformation of creation and the society in which we live. It is okay to get into politics. Politics is not a dirty word. It is okay to run for your city board and take your mercantile genes into that context. It is okay to become a doctor. Jesus may not come tomorrow, so be a doctor and your medical degree will serve as a framework for channeling your Melchizedek essence into creation while you are doing it in the spirit, moving from galaxy to galaxy and channeling it on earth in creation.

It is okay to get an engineering degree or be a tailor and make clothes for people because it is a manifestation of an incarnational reality of who God is in the world. Be a professor and train others in different types of knowledge while you are teaching the Gospel and or teaching children mathematics. While you move in the spiritual realm, help others become vessels for manifesting what you are doing in the spiritual realm. The Melchizedek Priesthood is an incarnational priesthood, but it plays out a cosmic principle. It functions in all diverse realms, dimensions, and dreams where God is doing great things. Be a builder and build houses that imbue the essence of Melchizedek with power. Be an architect and create buildings that reflect the beauty

of God in creation and sustain it. Be a righteous policeman. Plant vineyards and imbue them with the essence of God. It is time for the Melchizedek Priesthood to raise itself to the God level. The God who created came into the realm of creation and structured it to be a Melchizedek world. Let us call it the Melchizedek world order in which we all become the true embodiment of the Messiah in his pre-creation reality, creation reality, and creation unfolded reality.

Look at all the people we talked about and their access to divine provision in such an incredible way in their lives! I am not a prophet nor the son of a prophet, but I do realize that as you come into the Melchizedek Order, not only do positions open for you to be a vessel for the manifestation of divine transformation and transportation, but there is also an incredible opening to the movement of wealth. Creation bends towards you to bring divine provision. We can see the evidence in the way Jesus provided for the people and we see it in the way God provided for Israel in the wilderness. Everyone who walked in that dimension tended to come into some sort of sustainable and increased wealth.

It is not just about wealth, but about the supernatural divine provision that is available to us. The Melchizedek Priesthood is an attractor of abundance. Its vibration attracts abundance. Our High Priest, Jesus, told us clearly that He came so that we may have life and have it more abundantly. He said that He is the door through which we go in and out and find pasture[54] and that if we ask the Father in His name, we will receive.[55] He also said that we should ask for what we need so that the Father may be glorified through the Son.[56]

---

54 John 10:9-10
55 John 16:23
56 John 14:13

When we enter the fullness of the Melchizedek dimension, the realm of divine provision will be completely open to us. This includes the creation of wealth, which allows us to operate as kings on earth. A philosopher once said that it is not possible to be a true philosopher without wealth. The mark of the Melchizedek Order is that you begin to attract things. They begin to come to you. Not everything you attract will succeed, but everything you attract will be aimed at establishing you in your kingship so that you can reign with spiritual authority as well as the material authority for your situation.

You will notice that more and more believers are becoming aware of business and wealth opportunities because of the Melchizedek principle. Whenever the Melchizedek principle increases, wealth also increases. As we enter into the technological realm of what God is doing with us, God is giving us new sources of overflow. Abraham paid tithes, which opened up dimensions of creation, and after meeting Melchizedek, God said to him, "I am El Shaddai, I am your exceeding great reward. Walk towards my face and be fully complete."[57]

Melchizedek Sonship and Priesthood are becoming more prominent in this age, and we are shifting into a period where provision will not be limited to only certain individuals, but rather there will be a movement of provision within the body as a whole. Therefore, we need to be ready for the ideas that will come during this period. Get a pen and paper, get a journal, and start writing down your ideas. After this is finished, there will be a movement of wealth, and channels of provision will begin to flow. So, write down your ideas, brood over them, and allow them to receive the vibration of

57 Genesis 15

the Melchizedek gene that has been released into humanity by our Lord Jesus Christ.

You truly do have million-dollar ideas in your head and genes. You have the potential to attract and open realms of provision in your being, and your priesthood confirms this for you. Your High Priest stands in the place of divine provision and you have access to the door and the key to enter it. You have become a part of that realm because you are one with your High Priest. As a human being, you were not initiated into the Melchizedek Order, but rather God initiated Himself into your priesthood, serving as your High Priest. This ensures that God ministers through you to Himself, by Himself, and for Himself, and you receive the benefit of this divine ministration.

You are almost there, and the Lord is good. We should continue to look at people who have successfully tapped into the Melchizedek Order and transformed and transmitted their careers and periods of life, knowing that we can do it too. It is not just a theoretical idea, but something that real human beings have accomplished.

Chapter 7

QUESTIONS AND ANSWERS

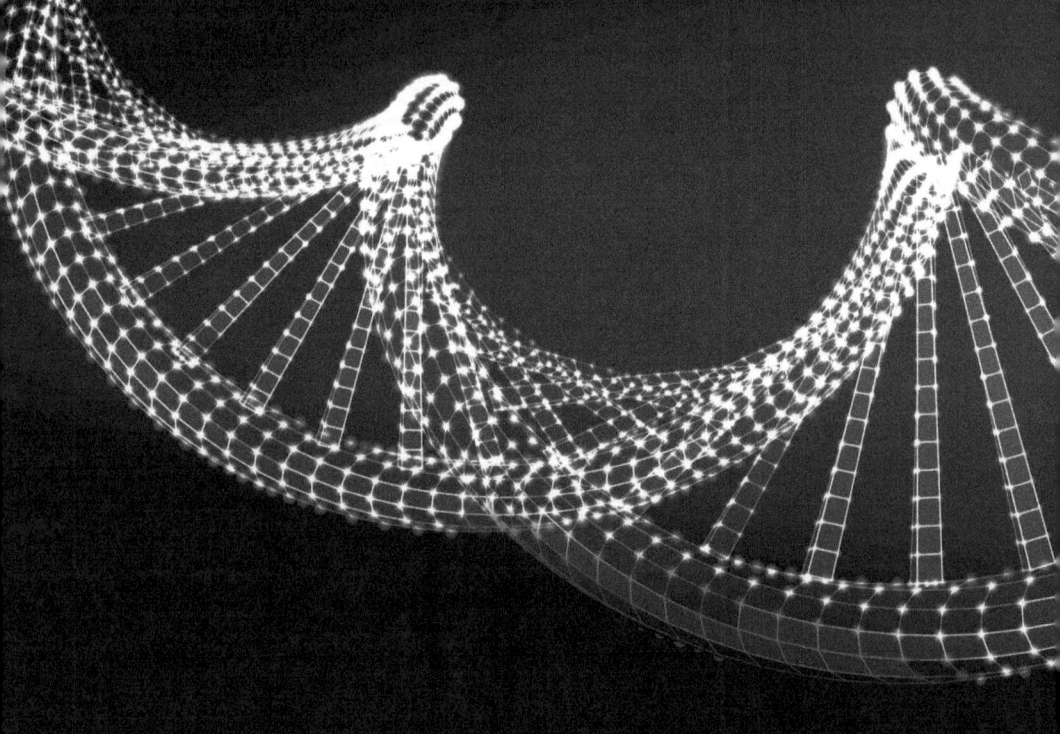

Does the Son of God minister to God as king
and priest in the living city of God or in the upper
temple, or is it a progression?

It is not a progression: it is immediate. The Son of God ministers to God as king and priest in both the living city of God and the upper temple simultaneously. The idea of sonship carries within it the concept of being a ubiquitous being, that is, wherever Christ is. This means that your ministration to God, even in ordinary things, becomes ministration in the Holy of Holies and in righteousness.

When you love someone as a Melchizedek Christian, you are directly ministering to God because, if they are the temple of God and you love them in the way that you do, that temple receives your worship as if God is receiving it. At the same time, if you move in the Spirit and are in the heavenly city worshiping God, you are ministering to all dimensions of the realm of the Father. Although you may think you are in one place in your mind, in reality, you are affecting diverse dimensions at the same time.

It is important to note that progression is seen only in terms of our minds and the development of our consciousness. As we grow in our understanding and connection with God, our consciousness expands and we begin to see ourselves as present in multiple dimensions. When we worship God, we are already in His presence, but our limited physical consciousness may not allow us to fully grasp this reality. The key to understanding this is to expand our consciousness and catch up with what we are in God. God is everywhere, and as we draw closer to Him, He draws us closer to Him.

Did we participate in the sacrifice of the Lamb of God who was slain before the foundation of the world or are we the archetype following the Order of Melchizedek?

The answer is both. We were part of the sacrifice of the Lamb of God because we were included in the archetype of humanity when it was carried out. At the same time, we also manifested it on earth, since both Jews and Gentiles condemned Jesus and the Romans carried out his crucifixion. Therefore, we participated in the sacrifice both as the archetypal Melchizedek principle in its original, pristine nature and as the priests (albeit from a terrible position) who took the life of the Son and released it into creation. The sacrifice had to be made by the priest, and it was done by human beings, or sons, including us. We participated in the sacrifice, but we are also beneficiaries of it because Jesus willingly gave himself in both cases.

If the Melchizedek Priesthood existed across all cultures of the earth since ancient times, should we assume that there are still those who have continued in the vocation of being priests outside of the traditional Christian religion until now?

I would not categorize it as being outside of the traditional Christian religion because doing so would create confusion. However, there are those who know the Lord and serve Him outside of the Judeo-Christian tradition. If they are truly part of the Melchizedek Priesthood, they will experience unity with the Messiah, who is the High Priest.

Not everyone knows the name of Christ, but those who reject idolatry and focus on the Most High and Eternal God are moving towards unity with the one new man, which cannot be completely diversified. Some people serve as priests while knowing God at that level, but they cannot be saved without the blood and without accepting the unity of the Melchizedek Priesthood in the Messiah, who is now the High Priest.

We must be careful because if there is idolatry involved, it is not truly the Melchizedek Priesthood. There are people in the midst of idol worship who reject idols and focus on the most High God, and when they hear the name of Christ, they recognize it as the name of the priest they have been worshiping. However, not everyone outside of Judeo-Christianity knows God or will know God simply by hearing the name. It is a matter of will and belief, and ultimately, Christ will reveal Himself to those who are searching for Him.

Is it true that as believers, if we leave our genetic physical DNA and all that lives on the earth, does this mean we are working towards the restoration of all things as many people of God are talking about?

No, it does not mean that unless you are referring to the restoration of creation as described in the book of Genesis. I do not see any scriptural or experiential evidence that suggests everything will be restored. We are working towards the salvation and redemption of human beings who then become the source for creation to see God and reveal the divine glory in it. If the restoration of all things includes the restoration of demons and the salvation of demons, I reject that idea because it is not scriptural. Scripture does not allow for the restoration of everything, including the things that need to be conquered. Jesus came to conquer, destroy, and deliver us from the hands of the devil, which had power over us and used the fear of death. Jesus came to remove death. The devil has been defeated, conquered, and his works destroyed. As for those who believe they supersede scripture, that is their gift and may God bless them with it. However, the church fathers have stated that Jesus did not become human to save all things but to save human beings. Through salvation, human beings become the restorers of the things that God created, starting from Genesis 1:5 onwards.

The answer is no if you mean the restoration of all things to include the restoration of Satan. I understand that this can be a controversial topic and it may cause people to talk about me, but I still love them. God is still God. Just because I believe their doctrine is false does not mean that I hate them. If someone were to approach me and say that Jesus Christ is not the Son of God, I would still love them, but that does not mean I would agree with their teaching. The problem with disagreement is that we tend to focus on our personal experiences and opinions rather than evidence and logic. However, our common mode of judging experiences should be based on the scriptures given to us.

A person may have a false doctrine but still have results because the results come from the grace of God, not from the doctrine itself. On the other hand, a person may have a perfect doctrine but not have any power manifesting from God. This does not mean that their doctrine is false because they do not have signs and wonders following them. We should not judge someone's experiences or doctrines based on the results they are seeing, but instead, we should focus on the truth and evidence found in the scriptures. We need to approach this topic differently. You may have many signs and wonders, but if your doctrine is false, it is not good. If you try to impose that false doctrine on others, they should reject it. However, it is important to acknowledge that God may still be using you. But never accept a false doctrine.

Let us consider William Branham as an example. None of these people can match William Branham in miracles, yet he went astray in his doctrine. Despite this, he is in heaven with God. However, he caused problems for people because their minds were tuned towards something that they should not have been. If you focus on satans and devils, how can you effectively minister to humanity without spreading some poison?

The restoration of all things does not include the restoration of demons and devils. The focus should not be on going to graveyards and doing things that the Bible explicitly tells you not to do. While it is important to know these things, it is not right to act on them. So, let us all be mindful of our actions.

There are doctrines that I have had to correct through my continuous study of scripture. Although I have had experiences, I do not always share them. Many of us want to appear relevant, so we often talk about our experiences just to be seen as important. However, this can be harmful to others if it leads to pride and a refusal to be corrected or challenged. We all need to be open to being questioned and challenged so that we can continually improve.

Recently, I was told by an unbeliever that I was complaining too much, and I had to take a step back and examine myself. What is wrong with people pointing out when something is not right? We should always be willing to examine our beliefs and actions. Just as Jesus allowed Himself to be judged by the Pharisees, even though He knew He could not be truly judged, He still engaged with them and rebuked them when they were wrong. He never stopped talking to them or the Scribes. He continued engaging with them because the purpose of engagement is to sharpen each other and bring each other closer to the truth that God has for us.

However there are truths that cannot be changed. If we say that Jesus Christ is just one of many ways, then we do not understand the point. If He is the Logos, then anyone who truly knows God will find their way to Christ. Anyone who is truly searching for the true God and not merely worshiping idols will find their way to God. God knows how to reveal Himself to people whose hearts are truly seeking Him. The Bible says that His eyes go to and fro over creation to find and prove Himself strong on behalf of those whose hearts are perfect before Him. Nobody can hinder God from doing that, and nobody can hinder God from revealing Himself to someone who is truly seeking Him.

I am not saying that the people who are preaching these things are not going to go to heaven. I never said that, and I never claimed to be more spiritual than they are. I just think their doctrine is incorrect and it does not matter how spiritual they may be, because we have the Bible text. You do not write the Bible. As wonderful as my books may be, they are not the Bible. They are inspired, but not at the level of the scriptures, at least not from the perspective of those who receive the scriptures.

I have heard people say that their experience is greater than the New Testament. Really! Based on what? I do love those people, but their statement is not supported.

If Melchizedek was in the mind of God and Adam was in the mind of God, Are they the same person?

When we say we are in the mind of God, who is actually in the mind of God? In the mind of God, we are present both as individuals and as an embodiment of His son, Jesus Christ. As part of the body of Christ, we stand in the presence of God in the mind of God. We are still individual embodiments of who Christ is, just as Adam became. So, Melchizedek was in the mind of God and was a manifestation of the person of Christ.

The body of Christ, of which we are a part, is the mind of God and is in fact a part of the Godhead. As believers, we are not just individuals who are a partial reflection of the being in the mind of God; we are a fullness of that being. It is a fractal principle where the parts are as big as the whole. You and I are not fragments of God's mind. We are the fullness of the mind of God, both as individuals and as the body of Christ. To separate it is to miss the point.

Melchizedek, as the prototypical priest, is in the mind of God. Melchizedek, as the manifestation of the created Adam, is in the mind of God. Melchizedek, as the High Priest, the son of God, is in the mind of God. We, who are priests in that order, are also in the mind of God. There is nothing outside of the mind of God if you really want to push it that far.

In summary, we are divinely entangled with Jesus Christ and are in fact in Him and He is in us. So, Melchizedek as the prototypical priest, the manifestation of the created Adam, and the High Priest, the son of God, are all in the mind of God, as are we who are part of the body of Christ and priests in that order.

Is pastoring a church a type of Melchizedek Priesthood?

Pastoring a church is not a type of Melchizedek Priesthood; it is a way of ministering and channeling the Melchizedek genes. The five-fold ministry is the fulfillment of the Melchizedek Priesthood. Any five-fold ministry that does not minister from a Melchizedek perspective is not a Melchizedek Priesthood.

Pastoring is a role that a believer can participate in and perform, but it is not the Melchizedek Priesthood itself.

The Melchizedek Priesthood is the fulfillment of the five-fold ministry and the harbinger of the new Adam being completely manifested. There is a mystery concerning our interaction and interconnection with one another that is still not fully understood. Being in Christ releases our whole being and opens up the depth of our being for access by all creation, except that which is anti-God or demonic.

Who actually took the knife and sacrificed the Lamb of God?

We are assuming that it was a knife, but it is different. I want to ask a question, "How does Jesus fight His war? Which sword does He use?" Do you see? He fights with the sword that comes out of His mouth. And how does He conduct His warfare? By the sword of His mouth. So, how do you think Melchizedek, the Lamb, had to be slain? It had to be by the word of humanity to release it. But in this realm, they could not just kill him. They had to shout, "Crucify him! Crucify him!"

It was not really the nails and the spears. The crucifixion happened by the condemnation issued at Pilate's palace. This given word released the death. So, Melchizedek had to speak a righteous word to release it into the space that God opened up so that creation could be sustained.

Remember, God did not tell Moses, "Strike the rock the second time." He said, "Speak to the rock." The sword of Melchizedek, or what you call the knife, is the word. It either gives life or it brings forth death. In the pre-foundation, the Melchizedek offering was a word of life, releasing life. In our realm, it was a word of death, causing death, which was then overcome by life. So, life and death are in the power of the tongue. Good question.

What was the reason that David didn't build the temple?

It was because his hands were filled with blood. God said that his hands were stained with blood, even though he fought against his enemies and even though he was killed for the purpose of defending the name of God. Yet, the shedding of blood by the implements of death was not completely acceptable to God. In other words, warfare by killing others and destroying others is not divine. It is not God's perfect will. And part of the reason is that every human being who is killed has a short-circuited capacity to accept God, and all kinds of things have to happen in the other realm for them to actually know God. Before the Messiah came, that was even worse. So if human beings kill each other, they do so because of their fallen nature, even though it might have been God's war. That tells you where God's heart is.

God did not want someone who had been shedding human blood to build His temple, sacrificing other people to build this kingdom. So God wanted a prince of peace. How did Solomon maintain peace in his reign? Mostly by talking to people. He had 40 years of peace in a place where David had wars every week. In fact, the name "Solomon" means peace, so he is a prince of peace.

So death and destruction are not the original will and the perfect will of God, and if we can keep our hands, from being stained with blood, we should. And it does not mean we do not defend, but we need to remember that even when we are justified in killing someone, it diminishes who we are. That is God's way of saying that.

In the world in which we live, wars must be fought now, but the goal is to achieve the Melchizedek Priesthood, where the prince of peace reigns over all. Even the most war-like religion believes in a place where there is no more war. So, I think that is part of it, but God told David, he could not build it because he was a man of war and his hands were stained with blood.

God said it; I did not say it. If we want to take scripture seriously, we cannot use our current ideological place to try to impose on scripture and to say things like wars are okay. They are not okay; they are a necessary evil in the world in which we live. Our goal is to one day have a Melchizedek Priesthood where Jesus Christ, our Lord, is king, and there are no more wars, no more death, no more sickness, and no more destruction.

It is what we teach and what we preach: no more of even this disagreement when we see as we are seeing, where we understand as we are understood when we know God in a way that does not divide us. It is coming.

How can the concept of the Melchizedek Priesthood be understood by an unbelieving spouse in marriage?

Before trying to teach the concept of the Melchizedek Priesthood to an unbeliever, the first step is to help them understand that they can be born again and become a priest of God. However, trying to teach these mysteries to an unbeliever before they have a relationship with Jesus may lead to difficulties. If the spouse is already practicing priesthood, then you can shape their understanding by pointing out that they are practicing this priesthood, but they need to know Jesus first for it to become fully embedded in them. Only if God directs you to do so should you teach these mysteries to an unbeliever. The key is to emphasize that being born again allows a person to become a priest of God and channel the divine power in creation.

The gospel message of Jesus Christ as the Messiah, the Son of God, and the Savior of the world is still essential. Jesus Christ is still the High Priest after the Order of Melchizedek, and preaching Him as such should be the focus. It is important to note the difference between a knee that bows because of belief and submission and a knee that bows due to conquest and rebellion.

About the Author

Adonijah Okechukwu Ogbonnaya (BA, MATS, MA, Ph.D.) is the founder of AACTEV8 International, an Apostolic and Kingdom Ministry that works with the Body of Christ across the globe for soul-winning, discipleship, training, and equipping the saints in Kingdom mysteries and Kingdom living. Located in Venice, California, Dr. Ogbonnaya (also known as A. Okechukwu or "Dr. O") has focused on helping believers engage the spiritual realities that have been opened up for them in the person of the Lord Jesus Christ.

He is a native of Nigeria, West Africa, and is Hebrew-born. He earned his Ph.D. in Theology and Personality and a Master's in Religion from Claremont School of Theology. He completed his M.A. in Theological Studies at Western Evangelical Seminary and his B.A. in Religion at Hillcrest Christian College in Canada. He also holds a Ph.D. in Business Publishing. Dr. Ogbonnaya is the presenter of numerous teachings found at www.aactev8.com.

Dr. Ogbonnaya is married to Pastor Benedicta and they are blessed with four wonderful children and grandchildren.

www.ingramcontent.com/pod-product-compliance
Lightning Source LLC
Chambersburg PA
CBHW051209120626
46547CB00013B/1278

* 9 7 8 1 9 6 4 9 5 9 1 6 0 *